The Korean State and Social Policy

International Policy Exchange Series

Published in collaboration with the
Center for International Policy Exchanges
University of Maryland

Series Editors
Douglas J. Besharov
Neil Gilbert

United in Diversity?
Comparing Social Models in Europe and America
Edited by
Jens Alber and Neil Gilbert

Child Protection Systems
International Trends and Orientations
Edited by
Neil Gilbert, Nigel Parton, and Marit Skivenes

The Korean State and Social Policy
How South Korea Lifted Itself from Poverty and
Dictatorship to Affluence and Democracy
Stein Ringen, Huck-ju Kwon, Ilcheong Yi,
Taekyoon Kim, and Jooha Lee

SCHOOL of
PUBLIC POLICY

The Korean State and Social Policy

How South Korea Lifted Itself from Poverty and Dictatorship to Affluence and Democracy

By

STEIN RINGEN

HUCK-JU KWON

ILCHEONG YI

TAEKYOON KIM

JOOHA LEE

OXFORD
UNIVERSITY PRESS

Published in the United States of America by Oxford University Press, Inc.,
198 Madison Avenue, New York, NY, 10016
United States of America

Oxford University Press, Inc., publishes works that further Oxford University's
objective of excellence in research, scholarship, and education

Library of Congress Cataloging-in-Publication Data

The Korean state and social policy : how South Korea lifted itself from poverty
and dictatorship to affluence and democracy / Stein Ringen . . . [et al.].
    p. cm. — (International policy exchange series)
Includes bibliographical references and index.
ISBN 978-0-19-973435-1 (hardcover : alk. paper)
1. Korea (South)—Social policy. 2. Korea (South)—Economic policy.
3. Korea (South)—Politics and government. 4. State, The 5. Democracy.
6. Welfare state—Korea (South) I. Ringen, Stein. II. Title. III. Series.
HN730.5.A8K657 2011
320.6095195—dc22   2010054129

1 3 5 7 9 10 8 6 4 2

Printed on acid-free paper
Printed in the United States of America

PREFACE

South Korea is a modern success story—a qualified success story, it is true, but in the end one of achievement. Where not long ago there was utter destruction and destitution, there is now affluence and freedom. The affluence remains poorly distributed and many have been left behind, and the freedom is protected by a democracy with many defects. But of achievement there has without question been much.

In this book, we follow a dramatic journey that has in many ways been a painful one for the Korean people. We would like to pay tribute to these people for their hard work, endurance, and dignity. The celebration of their ultimate success is also tempered by the sad and dangerous division of the Korean nation. It must be hoped that ways will be found to overcome the unnatural separation of Korea north and south.

The book we offer here is a political history of South Korea from 1945 to 2000. Our aim is that it will be read as a contribution in four areas of learning: on Korea specifically of course, but also on the power of social policy analysis as state analysis, on state theory, and to development studies.

It is a product of a program of doctoral studies in South Korean social and public policy at the University of Oxford. Kwon, Yi, Kim, and Lee all did doctoral research within this program, under the supervision of Ringen. The book builds on their dissertations by pulling their research together and bringing it up to date. It is in all respects a joint enterprise with all authors contributing to all parts. Primary responsibility has been distributed to Kwon for Chapter 2, Yi for Chapter 3, Kim for Chapter 4, Lee for Chapter 5, and Ringen for editorial coordination. For romanization of Korean words, we have followed the McCune–Reischauer system except for well-known names such as Syngman Rhee and Park Chung Hee.

We are grateful for much advice and assistance during the preparation of the book from Seok-Hyeon Choi, Sang Hun Lim, Yunjeong Yang, and Dayoon Lee, who have done subsequent research within the same program, and to Boya Shen and Prapaporn Tivayanond, who have done related research on social reform in China and Thailand respectively, also at the University of Oxford. Ja-young Yoo, Grami Dong, Hyungkyung Moon, and Woo-kyung Kim, all graduate students at the Graduate School of Public Administration of Seoul National University, provided invaluable assistance on quality control and consistency in the final text.

We are also gratefully indebted to the influence of Hyun-Chin Lim, the late Gordon White, and Thandika Mkandawire. Finally, we wish to express our thanks to Doug Besharov and Neil Gilbert, the series editors, for their support and guidance in bringing this project to fruition, and to Maura Roessner, Nicholas Liu, Tony Orrantia, and their colleagues at Oxford University Press.

CONTENTS

The Korean State and Social Policy

1

INTRODUCTION: THE BIRTH
OF THE STATE

There are two great mysteries in the political economy of South Korea. How could a destroyed country in next to no time become a sophisticated and affluent economy? And how could a ruthlessly authoritarian regime metamorphose with relative ease into a stable democratic polity?

Korean economic development has been, as is well known, state led. However, to make sense of that established wisdom, we need to understand in some detail how that state has worked and what kind of leadership it has provided. While authoritarianism was imposed with revolutionary means—two, arguably three, coups d'état—it ended without counter-revolution. Democracy did not require a dismantling of the state that had been built up during the dictatorship. There must be something in the structure of that state that enabled democratic rulers to take it over and readily work with it.

Very early, social policy became an indispensible instrument of rule. In turning their attention to social policy, it was as if the South Korean leaders looked to the more advanced industrial nations, saw there that the welfare state was a core instrument of rule, and said: that we too must have if we are to be an equal partner in the family of modern nations. President Chun, for example, on the inauguration of his presidency in 1980, conspicuously linked "the building of a welfare state" to "constructing an advanced country." We propose to disentangle some of the intricate complexities of the South Korean state through the prism of social policy, and by this avenue to have our say toward a resolution of the two great Korean mysteries. Ever since "the Iron Chancellor" Bismarck invented the modern welfare state in Germany in the 1880s, social policies have been

3

Table 1: South Korean Government Regimes

Tentative democracy (the First and Second Republics, 1948–1960 and 1960–1961)

　Syngman Rhee, civilian, elected president, 1948–1960*

　Yun Po-sŏn, civilian, president within a parliamentary government, 1960–1962

Hard authoritarianism (Military Government, 1961–1963)

　Park Chung Hee, military, Chairman of the Supreme Council for National Reconstruction, by coup d'état, 1961–1963

Soft authoritarianism (Third Republic, 1963–1972)

　Park Chung Hee, military, directly elected president, 1963–1972

Hard authoritarianism (Fourth and Fifth Republics, 1972–1981 and 1981–87)

　Park Chung Hee, military, indirectly elected president, 1972–1979

　Ch'oe Kyu-ha, civilian, indirectly elected president, 1979–1980**

　Chun Doo Hwan, military, coup d'état 1979, indirectly elected president, 1980–1988

Re-democratization (Sixth Republic, 1987–)

　Roh Tae Woo, military, directly elected president, 1988–1993

　Kim Young Sam, civilian, directly elected president, 1993–1998

Democratic consolidation (Sixth Republic, cont.)

　Kim Dae Jung, civilian, directly elected president, 1998– 2003

　Roh Moo Hyun, civilian, directly elected president, 2003–2008

　Lee Myung-bak, civilian, directly elected president, 2008–

* Syngman Rhee was elected president by the National Assembly in 1948, and by direct elections in 1952, 1956, and 1960.
** Ch'oe Kyu-ha was a stop-gap president under the control of the military junta.

recognized as, among other things, instruments of state building, rule, social control, order, efficiency, and legitimacy. Our analysis is in this tradition.

Table 1 lists the South Korean presidents and gives a simple typology of government regimes that will be used to organize the analyses that follow.

STATE CAPACITY AND SOCIAL POLICY GOVERNANCE

The story of South Korea from its birth in 1948 is one of dramatic modernization, both economically and politically. Economic modernization came first and is in the literature explained as "state led."[1] We think more detail needs to go into that explanation. Political modernization followed and has yet to find its proper explanation.[2]

To make sense of these mysteries, we will follow two narratives. The first one concerns social policy. We will lay out the development of social policy in detail and comprehensively, from its feeble roots in poor relief in the colonial period, early land reform, and the influx of foreign voluntary agencies in the first years of independence; to decisive initiatives in social insurance and occupational welfare, the "Koreanization" of the voluntary sector and the cultural revolution of the *Saemaul* Movements in the authoritarian period, and a gradually expanding inclusiveness of social insurance; and finally to important reforms of state provision in the aftermath of the East Asian economic crisis in 1997. Our aim here is to provide a complete picture of the origins, development, and timeline of the Korean welfare state and in the process to correct previous misunderstandings about how the welfare state emerged in this country. One such misunderstanding is that social policy has been peripheral and in any significant way a late result of economic advancement. We show that from early on it was a core component in the mode of state governance. Another misunderstanding pertains to the role of the voluntary sector, which has hitherto been seen as marginal and something that was given space late in the process and following re-democratization.[3] In fact, voluntary sector activity came very early and was the first major pillar of social protection in the young South Korean nation. It was not interrupted by authoritarian rule but rather stimulated, if controlled, and is as important in our first narrative as are the subsequent and more well-known initiatives of social insurance and occupational welfare.

Is South Korea a welfare state? Today, indisputably yes, but when did it become a welfare state? Since there is no single authoritative definition of "welfare state," the question is unanswerable. The seeds were sown early—the principle of compulsory social insurance was established within the Industrial Accident Insurance Act of 1963—and the welfare state as it stands today has come about gradually in a process from selective to inclusive protection.

Is it an East Asian welfare state? We classify it for most of our period as the arch-typical "developmental welfare state" which is associated with economic modernization in the East Asian "tiger" economies. Its developmental character was, however, gradually rolled back and, following the post-1997 reforms, has broken free from that mold—along with Taiwan but not other "tigers" that did not similarly reform—and become an unqualified welfare state that now differs very little from European-type welfare states in qualitative terms.

Our second narrative is about the Korean state and its shifting foundations in democracy, cronyism, *chaebŏl* capitalism, and dictatorship.[4] We follow it from the birth of the nation and through its development in successive republics and under a parade of sometimes colorful, outrageous, and admirable presidents; from democratic origins in 1948 via perverted democracy, failed democracy, soft authoritarianism, hard authoritarianism, and hesitant re-democratization; and finally to democratic consolidation after half a century. We find that much that has been lasting in the state's structure had come into place in the very early years and provided for a high degree of continuity through the subsequent turbulent shifts between authoritarianism and democracy. Throughout, including periods of harsh repression of trade unions and other movements, there was a constant demand and pressure for democracy from below that finally helped South Korea to consolidate as a democratic country in which democracy had been interrupted.

Our contribution here is mainly to the analysis of governance. There is ample material in the literature on the hard power aspect, but less systematically and in detail on just what kind of governance was delivered during and following the authoritarian period.[5] Bruce Cumings, for example, in *Korea's Place in the Sun*, follows South Korea's political history after 1960 as a story of hard power without much analysis at all of what the governments actually delivered by way of governance, and is thereby forced to downplay South Korea's national achievements and to ignore the great mysteries of how they could come about.

Both of these narratives are parts of the larger story of modernization and as such are worth laying out in their own right. However, our intention is not primarily to elucidate the respective roads to economic modernity and democracy, but to bring these two narratives together into an analysis of how they have interacted. If the state led the nation to economic modernization, just how did that come about? If democracy continued where authoritarianism let go, how could that happen? We believe the explanations must lie in how the state in its shifting incarnations has worked. And we think social policy is a good arena in which to observe what modern governments *do* and how they do it. What we are searching for in our social policy narrative is the governance part of our state narrative.

These analyses are informed by two basic ideas about how states work and about their effectiveness. The first idea is about the need to follow through from state structures to observing the *outcomes* of state action. In our social policy narrative, it is precisely such outcomes we identify and are able to use to explain the character of the South Korean state. The second idea is about the need to analyze power not only in terms of its magnitude but also, and more finally, by how it is used. In our state narrative, it is more the use of strength than strength itself that explains the nature of the leadership that pulled South Korea out of backwardness and into modernity.

South Korea took off to modernization in the authoritarian period. The authoritarian leaders turned to social policy as an instrument of rule. By bringing the social policy narrative into the state narrative in the authoritarian period, we can see that this state worked simultaneously in two very different ways. It was, on the one hand, a hard power state in the controlling of forces from below and, on the other hand, a soft power state in the way it dispensed governance throughout society—at least more of a soft power state than might have been expected from its more easily visible hard power manifestation.[6]

A satisfactory analysis of the authoritarian state in South Korea must incorporate its duality as a state that is strong in two very different ways, both in hard power force and in soft power governance. The authoritarian state was indeed a hard power state, but never *only* a hard power state. And in governance it had, or stumbled on, a keen awareness of the productivity of soft power.

This combined analysis leads us to a general conclusion about power and state leadership. Modernization was state led under authoritarianism, but not thanks to authoritarianism. It was not because the state had authoritarian strength that it was able to provide productive leadership, but because it used its power in a productive way. There is no support in our analysis for the theory that authoritarianism is conducive to development, but every support for the theory that state leadership, authoritarian or not, depends on the mode of governance. The authoritarian rulers in South Korea governed with more sophistication than has been the norm in authoritarian regimes. Hence, their state was not only a conventional power state, but also one with great capacity for practical governance. This is what explains both its effectiveness in driving forward economic development and the relative ease of transition when the underlying pressure for democracy could no longer be contained. Dismantling the hard power apparatus of the state still left the governance part intact—which the democratic rulers who came in when the authoritarian ones were overthrown could put to work for their purposes with little difficulty.

This book is about many things. It is about recent Korean history, it is about development and modernization, it is about dictatorship and democracy, it is about state capacity and governance, and it is about social protection and welfare states. Finally, it is a book about neither social policy nor state analysis, but about the interaction between the two. One of our aims is to lift social policy analysis out of the ghetto of self-sufficiency to which it is often confined and into the center ground of hard political science, where we think it belongs.

BACKDROP

In 1945, Korea started to rebuild itself as an independent nation, emerging from 40 years of Japanese colonization and the devastation of war. Being reduced first to a Japanese "protectorate" in 1905 and then formally a colony in 1910 had been traumatic for a proud nation with a history of independence reaching back perhaps fifteen hundred years. This experience came to strongly influence mindsets and events in the neo-independent Koreas, which both saw themselves on a mission to resurrect the nation.

To describe the Korean transition to modernity as unlikely is an extreme understatement. Late 20th-century South Korea was a nation that could not have been predicted 50 years earlier. It emerged from the ruins of war and civil war. It was an unwanted default result of the failure to hold the Korean nation united. It happened in a small and densely populated country with few natural resources.

It started under foreign overlordship and was initially carried forward in a decade of inefficient and corrupt governance. That gave way to 25 years of more or less military dictatorship, a dictatorship that, however and exceptionally, moved peacefully aside in favor of democracy.

At the end of the Second World War in the Pacific, and during the three initial years of American Military Government, two political camps emerged in Korea: a left–nationalist one with its base in guerrilla resistance against the Japanese in Korea, Manchuria, and China, and a conservative–nationalist one with its base partly in exile groups in the United States and elsewhere. In the jostling for power between these two camps and their patrons, Korea was rapidly *de facto* divided into two units, a division that was formalized with the creation of the Republic of Korea in August 1948 (with Syngman Rhee as president) and the Democratic People's Republic of Korea in September (with Kim Il Sung as the first premier and later president). Both were determined to see Korea unified under their own control and were sporting to bring this about by military means. By mutual provocation and counter-provocation, war broke out in June 1950 when North Korean forces attacked across the 38th parallel on the Ongjin Peninsula. The war lasted three years; pulled in other countries (principally the United States on the Southern side and China on the Northern side); was fought with brutality and atrocity on both sides; brought the world to the verge of nuclear war; cost millions of lives; destroyed landscapes, towns, and infrastructure; and ended in a stalemate with the two Koreas on either side of pretty much the same dividing line as before the war broke out.[7]

Both Koreas were allied with external powers, South Korea with the United States and North Korea with the Soviet Union and China. These alliances obviously influenced the respective national policies strongly, but not so as to make either of them puppet states. The Korean states, both in the North and the South, have been precisely *Korean* states, and their policies have been shaped by their own governments and not imposed from outside. Both Koreas as much used their patrons as they were used by them.

For 26 years from 1961, the country was governed autocratically until 1987, when it became a democracy again by force of free elections. With the 1997 elections, democracy was consolidated when the old guard gave way to leaders who did not spring from the authoritarian elite and the heroically tenacious opposition leader Kim Dae Jung was elected president.

The North Korean story we do not pursue here. In South Korea—which, for simplicity, we now mostly refer to as Korea—an evolution started after the war that resulted in the country first becoming an Asian "tiger" economically and then a full-fledged democracy. There was not much to build on: no democratic tradition, neither capital nor markets to speak of, and few natural resources. What it did have going for it was a population that, although worn down by war and misery, was comparatively well educated, work disciplined, and immersed in a Confucian culture of authority and respect. In addition, and importantly, there was *the state*, a state that was capable of taking hold of the economy that took off in the 1950s and stewarding it forward and upward. Without any doubt, the role played by what has been called *the developmental state*—highly interventionist with single-minded economic priorities—is entirely central to understanding the dramatic ascendance of East Asian countries in general and Korea in particular.

STATE AND SOCIETY

In the very birth throes of the nation, a pattern was introduced of pressure from below met by repression from above that was to be a constant in South Korean political life until the re-emergence of democracy more than 40 years later. The state emerged out of, on one side, the Committee for the Preparation of Korean Independence of what from September 1945 was called the Korean People's Republic, and, on the other side, also from September, the American Military Government.

The state became a Korean state in 1948. Syngman Rhee was elected president by the provisions of the democratic constitution of the First Republic. At the start there was freedom for opposition parties and the press. However, under the influence of what was soon a hegemonic, anti-communist ideology, the reality of Korean democracy was to erode. Still, the constitution remained democratic and the regime dependent on elections that the leaders could not fully control. The First Republic eventually collapsed under the pressure of mass demonstrations across the country in response to clumsy manipulations of the March 1960 elections and subsequent military and police brutality against the spreading uprising. That brought on the Second Republic, with a new and improved constitution and a system that, although short-lived, was established as a genuine democracy.

The state–society relationship in Korea can be seen as a tug-of-war between forces from below, in the form of popular constellations, movements, and organizations of various descriptions, and forces from above, in the form of the state, its apparatus of control and governance, and its partners in big business. That relationship has been a shifting one, regulated by the absolute strength of the competing parties and by their strength relative to each other.

Forces from above were obviously dominant during the authoritarian periods, but they also remained strong with the re-introduction of democracy. The state, authoritarian or democratic, has been at the center of political, economic, and social life, in different ways and degrees, clearly but continuously the dominant source of national leadership. And in the state, authoritarian or democratic, the presidency has been the central and leading institution. This structure—a state-led society and a president-led state—informs Korean political analysis generally, as it does the present analysis.

Tentative Democracy

Korea was liberated in 1945 by Japan's surrender to the Allied Powers after the destruction of Hiroshima and Nagasaki by atomic bombardment. The legacy of colonization and war was social and political disarray and massive and oppressive poverty.

President Syngman Rhee's priorities were the establishment of a capitalist market economy and an anti-communist state. He came to power within a democratic order, but the preservation of that order was not much of a concern for the Korean elite or their American patrons.

The Korean War was to define state–society relations during the First Republic. In its wake, Rhee turned anti-communism into the official regime ideology and a basis for discrediting and persecuting anything of a leftist slant in civil society. He strengthened further the state apparatus of bureaucratic authoritarianism, which he inherited from the American Military Government and which it in turn had taken over from the Japanese colonizers. Popular movements remained active, but energies were constrained primarily to family and clan affairs devastated by the war and thus away from political life and from the building of alliances that might have challenged the state. From a height of political power immediately following the civil war, the regime gradually lost credibility and energy until it collapsed in the *April Revolution* in 1960, when it by its own machinations provoked forces from below back into the public space in violent nationwide demonstrations, and the ageing president, now 85 years old, lost the backing of even the Americans.[8] He won his third popular election in March 1960 but was forced to resign in April and to leave the country for exile in Hawaii.

The economy in ruins, Korea initially depended massively on foreign assistance. Reconstruction and stabilization programs were financed mainly by the United States. By the late 1950s the Korean economy was firmly embedded in the U.S.-led international capitalist system.

The Korean state was not a particularly impressive one during the First Republic, but in hindsight surprisingly much was set in stone in that period with effects that have carried on in Korean life. First, Korea was, again, born democratic, and the First Republic established democracy as the rightful system for Korea. Second, it was from the start a state-centered society. Third, state and government were dominated by the strong presidency. Fourth, the economy was made the priority of national development, if at first with much dithering, inconsistency, and inefficiency. Fifth, a quasi-monopolistic capitalist economy started to emerge that was later consolidated with a relatively small number of large conglomerates, the *chaebŏl*, at its center. Sixth, the economy itself was state-led within a strong symbiotic relationship between government and big business. Seventh, voluntary agencies crowded into the vacuum of government non-provision of social services. And finally, a system of governance whereby the

state, although strong, worked with and through non-state actors for the implementation of government intentions. In the field of social policy, voluntary agencies were to become the state's instruments of social service delivery and
businesses its instruments of social security. We are at the creation of the nation
and it was created in ways that have endured through shifting political fortunes
and to this day.

A notable achievement of the First Republic was land reform, which had
started under the American Military Government in 1946 and was completed in
1955, and which paved the way for economic advancement in later periods.[9]
Absentee ownership was mostly abolished and land holding limited to small
properties. The government bought out larger land owners and sold land to former tenant peasants at subsidized prices. This brought down the old land-owning
class and ended its political influence, and created a new class of self-owning
farmers. Agricultural productivity increased, rural poverty was reduced, and
farmers were able to send their children to school. This resulted in a nearly over-
night revolution of education. By the late 1950s, the rate of literacy had reached
almost 90 percent of the total population. A huge reservoir of educated labor
emerged to pour into the industrial take-off.

With the collapse of the First Republic, democracy reasserted itself in the
Second Republic following free elections in July 1960. That was to fail, but the
experience provided tangible evidence of the underlying pressure for democracy
that was ready to rear its head when given space. Subsequent authoritarian rulers
were no doubt aware and fearful of that constant pressure and went to great
lengths to contain it.

The Second Republic made "economic development first" its priority. On this
nothing has subsequently changed. When President Lee Myung-bak took office
on February 25, 2008, "economic revitalization" was again the guiding priority
for the domestic agenda in a language that would have been familiar 50 years
earlier.

The Second Republic was democratic but unable to rule. In particular, it was
unable to control the military, which had come out of the Korean War as the
country's strongest institution and had gained in strength from the subsequent
mesh of anti-communist fears and quasi-repressive state maneuvers. It had
become a military in which strong elements were persuaded of their destiny
to lead.

Authoritarianism
With the military coup led by General Park Chung Hee and a following of colo-
nels in 1961, democracy was suspended in Korea for 26 years, although it was
allowed some space of operation during the interim Third Republic. The state
overpowered society, articulated modernization in the form of economic growth
as the national project of absolute priority, and mobilized all relevant forces to

advance that purpose. Although the state was firmly in command, authoritarianism oscillated from hard to soft depending on both shifting government policies and inclinations and the extent of power mobilized by forces from below.

Park had his military education in the Japanese army and had fought on the Japanese side in Manchuria until the end of the Pacific War in 1945. He joined the new American-formed army in Korea but was dismissed dishonorably after having been involved in an attempted "communist" inspired rebellion. He was reinstated at the outbreak of the Korean War and fought against the communist North. He subsequently rose to the rank of Major General, came to power in the bloodless coup in 1961, and stayed in power until he was killed in 1979. He remains an enigmatic figure, reportedly a devout Buddhist but with his deep convictions and ideas unknown. While in power he held great personal authority, and the Third and Fourth Republics were in a very real sense *his* system.[10]

The coup makers were motivated by what they saw as an avalanche of accumulated problems: the Second Republic's ineffective governance, unruly public demonstrations, and the spread of radical ideologies. For two years they ruled through a military junta, the Supreme Council for National Reconstruction. In 1962, they drafted a new constitution that, inspired by that of the First Republic, re-emphasized a strong presidency and a weak legislature and included wide-ranging limitations on political activity. The Third Republic was launched and Park elected president. This ushered in a period of soft authoritarianism in which politics was played out under a constitution that did not explicitly contradict democracy, although not softer than to resort to martial law when necessary, as for example already in 1964.[11]

The domination of society by the authoritarian state culminated in 1972 in the *Yushin* (meaning revitalization) constitution, which brought hard authoritarianism back, effectively in a second coup d'état, although a coup within a coup. Park again declared a state of martial law, dismissed the National Assembly, closed universities, enforced strict censorship of the media, prohibited civic organizations from involvement in political advocacy, and limited the availability of strikes and lockouts in the labor market.[12]

The dictatorship sought legitimacy in anti-communism—in part a smokescreen for keeping the lid on threatening forces from below—economic modernization, efficiency, and social policy. The powerful drive for economic development dramatically transformed Korean society and economy, scaling back agriculture, building up big business, and creating a new middle class headed by a small and powerful capitalist elite. Various welfare-related laws were passed, although only a few programs were actually put into effect, most of them confined to accommodating administrative and security bureaucracies of the state itself.

Park revolutionized Korean politics for the good as well as the bad. He legalized autocracy and eventually no-nonsense military dictatorship. He maintained order with violence, repression, and brute force. He articulated and made explicit the modernization project. He introduced effective governance and gave the great transformation of Korean society direction and force. He developed further and perfected the state's apparatus of bureaucratic authoritarianism but also the system of governing through state–business and state–voluntarism coalitions. He launched and maintained a campaign of mass mobilization for self-reliance in rural and industrial populations in the *Saemaul* Movements. He launched the welfare state. His was the period of the developmental state in its pure form.

It is in no way surprising that he included welfare state initiatives in his portfolio of rule. President Park was in the business of nation building and state formation, but of doing that with no obvious right to be in power. He was, not unusually, a social reformer for decidedly non-social ends. What is worthy of note is not so much that he spoke and to some degree acted on "welfare," but rather that he had the ability to understand that his project of modernization needed pillars to stand on in addition to power.

Park's assassination in October 1979 left a political vacuum that caused the *Yushin* system to temporarily break down and enabled democracy to show its face again. The premier, Ch'oe Kyu-ha, a civilian, became interim president in December, proclaimed his government to be transitional, and promised an early revision of the *Yushin* constitution and a return to a democratic order. But it was not to be. The generals intervened again with yet another military coup, first putting Ch'oe under administration after only a few days in office and then, following bloody repressions of violent civil demonstrations, in May 1980 declared martial law, dissolved the National Assembly and political parties, deposed Ch'oe and his government, replaced it with a Special Committee for National Security Measures, and issued various repressive orders against popular movements. The leader of this second coup, General Chun Doo Hwan, was elected president in August under the provisions of the *Yushin* constitution, undertook symbolic constitutional reform that technically ended the *Yushin* system, and had himself re-elected in 1981.

President Chun was never able to exercise Park-like total control, and the developmental state started, if first imperceptibly, to crumble. The number of student demonstrations increased year by year, as did the number of trade unions and labor disputes. Student, labor, religious, and other civil groups became more organized, such as in the Council of Movements for People and Democracy and the National Council for Democracy and Reunification, both established in 1984, leading to the National Movement Headquarters for a Democratic Constitution in early 1987. Even so, he was able to secure the continuation of authoritarian rule. He did this in part with the help of three proactive measures: social purification, economic stabilization, and new welfare state initiatives.[13]

Under the slogan "the realization of a just society," he launched a campaign that combined, on the one hand, measures against criminal and broadly interpreted decadent social elements, and on the other hand confiscation of illegally gained assets during the Park years by members of the civil service and the business class. In the economic domain he distanced himself from what was seen as excesses of the Park era and introduced measures to curb inflation, improve export performance, and reduce unemployment. In this he was fortunate and was able to deliver noticeable economic progress.

Finally, he pledged the Fifth Republic to the "building of a welfare state." His revised constitution included a clause that "the state should bear responsibility for promoting social security and social welfare." This rhetoric was promoted strongly and skillfully from the beginning of the new republic, but the reality remained that social policy initiatives were hesitant and, as previously, subordinate to the overriding concern of economic progress. The state might take initiatives in the area of social welfare, but delivery would remain in the hands of non-state actors. The new welfare rhetoric did, however, come with a new emphasis on the role of social services in addition to social security. The knock-on effect was that while "welfare" had hitherto been seen as predominantly a matter of occupational welfare for the state–business coalition, it now became more explicitly recognized as a matter for, in addition, the state–voluntarism coalition. ("Voluntarism" is a slippery concept in a setting of authoritarian rule, but still the best available concept to capture the activity of associational non-state actors during the entire period we are observing.)

Re-Democratization

The run-up to presidential elections in late 1987 finally brought on the transition from authoritarianism to democracy, and with it the rolling back of the developmental state. Early in the year, President Chun announced that there would be no revision of the constitution and that the presidential election would as previously be indirect, which is to say under his own control. However, the opposition was now better organized, and this announcement resulted in nationwide demonstrations with broad participation, a participation that broadened yet more following the death of two student demonstrators. This *June Uprising* forced the regime to concede constitutional reforms. The establishment candidate committed himself to democratic elections, first of the president in December 1987 and then of the National Assembly in April 1988.

Paradoxically, however, the establishment candidate, Roh Tae Woo, who had been one of Chun's co-conspirators in the 1980 coup, was elected, and Korea was stuck with yet another general-turned-president. (The period of military leadership was hence to last from 1961 to 1993, and to outlast authoritarianism by six years.) He won just over a third of the vote, but the opposition was split and out-maneuvered itself. In 1990, Roh succeeded in forging a "grand conservative coalition" with two opposition parties, creating a solid ruling majority in the National Assembly and leaving the democratic opposition proper, Kim Dae Jung and his Party for Peace and Democracy, isolated.

In response to this reinforcing of conservative forces from above within the democratic framework, civil society groups remobilized and resumed their pro-democracy campaigns. From their perspective, Roh's regime was now a form of liberalized authoritarianism.

The next presidential election, in 1993, resulted in the election of yet another candidate who had committed himself to the conservative establishment coalition, Kim Young Sam. He was, however, also the first civilian president for more than three decades and had been on the opposition side in the authoritarian period. He initiated various political and democratic reforms and succeeded in reducing anti-government civil mobilization. However, his power base remained the conservative coalition that Roh had forged.

Democratic Consolidation

From 1987 to 1997, the Korean state was schizophrenic: the structure was democratic, but the strong presidency was in the hands of the old guard. Although the dictatorship was broken, authoritarian attitudes and practices lingered. In principle, democracy was reinstated with the 1987 settlements, but in practice it re-emerged through a gradual process up to 1997.[14]

Kim Dae Jung was an advocate and activist of democracy from during the regime of Syngman Rhee. A catholic, he was elected to the National Assembly in 1963. In 1971 he was chosen as the presidential candidate of the New Democratic Party and, with 46 percent of the vote (in spite of election rigging by the ruling party), nearly defeated President Park. He stood in the presidential elections again in 1987 and 1992, and was finally elected in 1997. During the dictatorship, he suffered imprisonment, house arrest, exile, several attempts on his life, kidnapping from abroad by the security forces, a charge of treason, and a death sentence, until he was cleared of all charges in 1987. He was awarded the Nobel Peace Prize in 2000 and died in 2009.[15]

Compared to all previous presidents, Kim Dae Jung was obviously to the left, but he was not a radical and certainly not a socialist politician. He continued the tradition of economic development in a capitalist system. The change that was brought on with the "people's government" in 1997 was rather that the constant confrontation between forces from above and forces from below was superseded. The state had been made democratic and was now taken over by a leader with democratic credibility. Public policy came to be formulated in processes in which forces from below were normally integrated and participating. The developmental state had run its course.

Democratic consolidation coincided with the East Asian economic crisis, which hit Korea severely and resulted in, among other problems, widespread unemployment. President Kim committed his administration to three priorities: democracy, market economy, and what he called "productive welfare." The latter signaled a new understanding of the role of the state with a stronger recognition than previously of social and citizenship rights. That translated into a commitment, although not entirely clear and explicit, to a state-guaranteed social minimum.

That again followed through to new social assistance programs in which the state took on broader responsibilities of provision. The Korean welfare state has continued to be predominantly based on the politics of regulation, but its extension into the politics of provision made it a new and broader kind of welfare state.

OUTLINE

In Chapter 2, we start our analysis in the paradox of dictatorial social reform and the introduction of social security as an instrument of rule. We lay out the development and structure of the Korean welfare state. In Chapter 3, we turn to the state–business coalition of occupational welfare and the muted drama of capital, labor, and class conflict. In Chapter 4, we follow on to the state–voluntarism coalition of social service delivery. We see there more vibrancy in Korean civil society even during the authoritarian period than Korean historiography has tended to recognize. Finally, in Chapter 5 we encounter the coincidence of democratic consolidation and economic crisis and the surprising expansion rather than contraction of welfare state governance that was to result.

2

THE STATE MEETS MODERNITY

Not surprisingly, in a nation reinventing itself, the state started hesitantly. Surprisingly fast, however, it became a state with a mission.

MODERNIZATION

There is obviously no simple explanation of the unlikely South Korean transition. But the first part of the explanation is found in the legacy of colonialism. Korean national history in the 20th century can be divided neatly into two periods: first, up to 1945, the humiliation of colonization; and second, after 1945, the resurrection of the nation from humiliation. Events in the second period were dictated by a mission of regaining what Bruce Cumings has called "Korea's place in the sun." That mission was shared by what were to become South and North Korea, although they went about it in very different ways. In the South it was a shared project of state and society and of shifting governments. There were strong disagreements about how to articulate the project and how to advance it in practice, but there was at the core a shared project. This idea of *mission*, then, was the constant undercurrent in government ambitions and actions all through the second part of the 20th century.

Korea has been an unruly polity—one of rather dramatic shifts back and forth in power relations and not one that readily lends itself to being described with terms such as *continuity* and *consensus*. But beneath the often dramatic roller coaster of trials and tribulations, there was nevertheless a basic continuity of consensus over a shared ambition of national resurrection.

There was to be a great deal of authoritarianism in both parts of Korea, but whether in the North or the South and however brutal, not authoritarianism for merely self-serving purposes. Korean authoritarianism has been authoritarianism with a project. That can be stated without qualification for South Korea. While in the North authoritarianism became entrenched and—with the person cult of Kim Il Sung—arguably moved from authoritarianism for a purpose to authoritarianism for its own sake, in the South authoritarianism had the good fortune to collapse before it could pervert into making itself its own purpose. South Korean authoritarianism is intriguingly complex, and its analysis must be strongly informed by the undercurrent of the project to which it was bound.

A further part of the explanation is that the national project in South Korea came to be formulated as a progressive one. The new Korea was to find its place in the sun not by looking back to some former glory, but by looking forward to industrial modernization. While in the North the project came to be interpreted as a nostalgic one of recreating a self-sufficient and even isolated Korea, in the South it was clearly and explicitly seen as one of *modernization*.[16] South Korea was to be an industrial economy—open, capitalist, anti-communist, respected, and an integrated partner in what was then the Western camp. This was a contested interpretation of the national project, and at times resisted by various forces from below, but was nevertheless the one that prevailed to give direction to the nation's development.

The South Korean state has been a strong state. Its tradition of bureaucracy goes back to the *Koryŏ* Dynasty in the tenth century when the meritocratic system and central control of local provinces were first established. The modern strong state was in part a colonial legacy. "The strong colonial state, the multiplicity of bureaucracies, the policy of administrative guidance of the economy, the use of the state to found new industries, and the repression of labor unions and dissidents that always went with it provided a surreptitious model for both Koreas in the post-1945 period. Japan showed them an early version of the 'bureaucratic–authoritarian' path to industrialization, and it was a lesson that seemed well learned by the 1970s."[17]

But it was also a specifically South Korean invention. Up until about 1960, the expectation, at least outside of Korea, was that the South was not likely to become seriously economically viable and would probably fall back to some kind of domination by Japan. The centrally engineered process of development by, as we shall see, a combination of ruthlessness and prudence under the auspices of the strong state was homemade and imported from nowhere. Both Koreas have been strong state systems, but the specific character of the South Korean brand of strong statism stands in sharp relief against the uncompromisingly heavy handed version in the North.

The strong state part of the South Korean story needs, however, to be put in perspective in several ways. If the meaning of *strong state* is a state that is capable of delivering effective governance, then that came with the military coup in 1961 and has persisted ever since. But if the strong state is identified by state domination and society subordination, the Korean state has not been universally strong. First, the strong state in this meaning came only with the military dictatorship and lasted no longer than to 1987 with the re-emergence of democracy. Furthermore, already during the last part of the military dictatorship, from 1980 to 1987, the state started to lose its grip and a somewhat more balanced relationship between state and society to emerge. In fact, dictatorial control had started to slip already under Park when the Korean economy deteriorated toward the end of the 1970s and opposition and labor movements were emboldened to mount protests and take to the streets. The winding down of authoritarianism happened in a gradual process that also lasted into the period of re-democratization after 1987 so that a new equilibrium of state subordination to society was only settled in 1997 with the consolidation of democracy. And further again, even during the initial period of authoritarianism from 1961 to 1979, it was only in 1972, with the introduction of the *Yushin* constitution, that President Park made the state unequivocally strong. When he normalized his reign in 1963, he did that in a quasi-democratic manner. Already in his first election, in 1963, he had a brush with the possibility of losing. In 1971 he came near to losing again and drew the conclusion that he could put no trust in gratitude and would have to depend on force to be able to continue to rule.

Secondly, if we locate the Korean strong state to the reign of President Park, we need to introduce yet another nuance even during that period. Although Park's state was without question strong in the meaning that it dominated society, it was also a state that renounced some of its strength in favor of society in the interest of being able to rule for what it saw to be its purpose.[18] It dominated, but not as uncompromisingly as its strength would have allowed. It could have put the main actors on the side of society under command, but instead it opted for co-optation and cooperation, in particular with the business and voluntary sectors. It ruled by deciding what should be done but then delegating to non-state actors to get it done. This state could have ruled differently. It could have turned South Korea more uncompromisingly into a command economy and command society, if not of a communist kind then of a more fascist leaning. Other military regimes did so at the time and have done so later, as for example in the case of Burma. But it did not; it chose to not take the degree of control over society that it had the power to do.

This was not inevitable; it was a chosen strategy by a power elite that could have acted differently. The reason for this relative restraint in a brutal regime was that it had bound itself to the mission of modernization. It had the power to subdue society more fully—and its leaders were no doubt by instinct so inclined—but had it done so it would have had to sacrifice modernization for control. Many authoritarian regimes have done just that with no hesitation. A blatant example is that of President Mugabe in Zimbabwe. But the Korean state did not go down that route. The regime committed itself to modernization and made that its *raison d'être*. By that commitment it cut off from itself any avenue of action that would have seriously compromised its purpose. The elite in power were able to understand, or at least act as if they understood, that modernization could not be achieved by command alone. They would need the more or less willing cooperation of non-state actors that they could not put fully under command without rendering them ineffective for their purpose. Their governments thereby found themselves dependent on non-state actors for the delivery of a part of the governance that they needed to get delivered, and thereby again, for all their strength, found themselves in a sense at the mercy of those on whom they depended for governance. It is easy to observe the brutality of the Korean authoritarian state, but in this case, to truly understand the character of the state in this period, we need also to include the more difficult observation of non-action, of what it could have done but chose not to do.

The military coup in 1961 brought *two* experiences to Korea: on the level of rule it brought dictatorship, and on the level of governance it brought effectiveness. Like it or not, the authoritarian rulers took hold of the nation and steered it forward. The counterfactuals are unknown. Korea might have modernized without a dictatorial state. The military rulers might have produced effective governance with less ruthless means. On these matters we cannot pronounce. What is however descriptive fact is that Korea did modernize and that it in formative periods was ruled autocratically.

President Park's rule came to an end when he was killed in 1979. He had intended to continue to rule, possibly for life, something he had made provisions for in the *Yushin* constitution. We cannot know what would have happened had he been able to continue, and it is entirely possible that he would have come to sacrifice modernization for absolute and continued power. But that was not put to the test, and South Korean authoritarianism was for as long as it persisted constrained by a purpose beyond itself.

If authoritarianism is the first core issue in the Korean story, democracy is the second. The Korean state was born democratic, and democracy is a constant in Korean political life during our period—democratic origins, democratic pressures, and democracy in action. From the very moment that peace broke out on August 15, 1945, society made its presence felt in Korean political life. Within days, trade unions and peasant movements mushroomed and launched into militant action in strikes, demonstrations, people's committees, village self-government, and land and plant seizure. By November 1945, there were nearly 1,200 trade unions in the country and a General Council of Korean Trade Unions on the national level. Peasant unions came together in the General League of Korean Peasants. The Democratic National Front was the vanguard political organization of labor and peasant movements.

It is not easy to explain this sudden eruption of spontaneous action from below in a country without democratic traditions, but this is what happened— and it was over the years to happen again and again. At critical junctures, a desire for democracy asserted itself forcefully when it could. This desire would be suppressed repeatedly but never killed. South Korea has been a democratic polity in which democracy in periods has been repressed. It did not become a democracy in 1987; it was a democracy in which democratic government re-emerged in 1987 and was consolidated in 1997.

Authoritarianism and democracy, then, are the organizing principles in our analysis, but there is a difference. The story of authoritarianism is highly dramatic. It was introduced at the infancy of modernization and shaped the nation. The story of democratic consolidation is more one of normality. It was achieved gradually with the maturity of the nation when it was—in all respects except the political—already modern.

THE STRONG STATE

The military coup in 1961 created a new regime and made Park Chung Hee its undisputed leader. He was not the originator of the conspiracy or the brain behind it. That honor falls on Kim Chong-p'il and a group of serving and retired (mostly junior) army officers. Park was recruited into the conspiracy at a later stage as one of very few generals untainted by political corruption under the Syngman Rhee government and thereby as a suitable figurehead for the rebellion. He joined in, but as it turned out far from as a mere figurehead.

After the coup he served as vice-chairman and soon chairman of the Supreme Council for National Reconstruction until he was elected president in 1963. The new regime had an urgent need to give itself legitimacy. In its first year it published a Five Year Economic Plan in which it presented the coup as a "revolution of economic independence." By 1963, ahead of the presidential elections, Park was able to give his idea of purpose, project, and priority a clear articulation:

> "I want to emphasize and reemphasize that the key factor of the May 16 Military Revolution was in effect an industrial revolution in Korea. Since the primary objective of the revolution was to achieve a national renaissance, the revolution envisaged political, social and cultural reforms as well. My chief concern, however, was economic revolution."[19]

This was a government that justified itself by a commitment to a clear formulation of purpose and to advancing that purpose more effectively than the alternative it had overthrown. It claimed a right to be in power by force of its ability to deliver the modernization the nation desired.

President Park Chung Hee was the overpowering personality in South Korean politics in the second part of the twentieth century, with no equal in power, ruthlessness, or longevity. He was the creator of the strong state, shaped the country for good and bad during his reign, and profoundly influenced future developments. He came to power in a military coup and eliminated the short-lived democratic Second Republic. He rigged and re-rigged the constitution to enable himself to rule the country as long as he wanted. He let himself be elected and re-elected through processes could hardly be called elections and installed National Assemblies under his control. He declared martial law when it suited him and held on to and exercised power with the help of violence, repression, and a vast secret police under his command. He established a huge presidential bureaucracy that controlled every detail of public policy. He stayed in power for eighteen years until he was killed by his own intelligence chief in 1979, possibly in a drunken brawl.

Yet no sooner had he made himself dictator than he started to build the Korean welfare state. Not until under his successor, Chun Doo Hwan, was the concept of "welfare state" introduced officially, but the basic initiatives were taken by Park. Industrial Accident Insurance was introduced in 1963; National Health Insurance in 1965 as an experimental program, gradually becoming compulsory as of 1977; poor relief improved as of 1963; a National Pension Act adopted in 1973, although not implemented during Park's reign; and civil service and military pensions introduced in 1962 and 1963.

In addition, there was a conspicuous case of non-action on the part of a dictatorial government. Since independence, a network of voluntary agencies had been operating on the social scene in Korea, notably in the delivery of social care and services. Voluntary agencies are the fabric of civil society. One might have expected the new dictators to turn against what was becoming a sophisticated voluntary sector or to rein in its activities. They did not, however. They regulated the sector but allowed it to continue to work and to flourish, and it made itself dependent on non-government associations for the delivery of social services.

The picture of a hard state being dependent on a network of soft agencies is more nuanced than the conventional strong state picture of the Korean polity. The unfolding of the story of Korean voluntarism has contributed importantly to the interpretation in this book of the specific character of the strong Korean state. That interpretation starts with showing that the state–business relationship was never a straightforward one of command and obedience but a more symbiotic one. It continues with the discovery that there was also a similar symbiotic relationship between the state and the voluntary sector. Voluntary association networks are dangerous for any authoritarian state. An authoritarian state has many natural enemies, but most of those—those that can be identified and singled out—it can usually manage with relative ease. A structure of voluntary agencies is a different animal, not an identifiable enemy but more of, from the regime's point of view, a threatening cancer in the body politic. The strong Korean state, in need of legitimacy and therefore of having services delivered, was forced to allow this cancer to spread in its own organism. This goes some way toward explaining how democracy could take over from authoritarianism in a smooth process. Once the authoritarian grip was gradually relaxed, Korean civil society was there, ready to stand up and far from lost or helpless.

Why did Park Chung Hee make himself a pioneer of social reform? The answer to this question is quite complicated. It was certainly not because he was dedicated to social reform for the sake of social justice. He introduced social reform because he saw it to be useful for other purposes to which he was dedicated. But those purposes were complex, including at least (1) to stay in power, (2) to be able to govern and to execute rule effectively, and (3) to promote the revolution of economic growth.

Confrontation has been a constant theme in Korean politics: government power challenged and subjected to conflict from below, often strongly and often militantly, always unruly. Holding on to power in this environment is a battle. In the authoritarian period it was done by force and violence. But the preservation of power and the ability to use it also needed something else, some element of legitimacy to justify itself. President Park was not a man to hesitate with the use of repression when he saw that it was called for and useful, but he was also able to recognize that force and repression were on their own a tenuous basis for power. One reason he turned to social reform was that he was not satisfied to rely exclusively on control. He felt a need to also use "kind and gentle" policies, which would give him and his regime some aura of political acceptability.

Hence, he was a cynical and self-serving social reformer. He launched social reforms and gave people some social security, or some semblance or feeling of security, because that made it easier for him to rule over them as he wanted. That was one reason, but only one. The idea that social reform is used as a means of regime legitimacy is correct and central to our story, but is still not the be all and end all of understanding the complicated machinations of Korean politics in this period. It is without a doubt true that Park was dedicated to staying in power, that he indeed would have clung on for longer had he not been killed, that nothing in his politics was divorced from his instinct to preserve and perpetuate his own power, and that he was willing to use any means to stay in power. There was nothing intrinsically "kind and gentle," then, about this politician. All of that is true.

But there was still more to it. President Park was dedicated, in addition to holding on to power, to the *use* of power. He was in it for something in addition to himself. He saw himself to be, and was, an agent of modernization and of the restitution of the Korean nation in South Korea. That was his mission and that is what he wanted to use power for.

He argued that South Korea for this purpose needed authoritarian rule, at least for a while. That was needed to impose on this unruly and underdeveloped country the unity of purpose, determination, and discipline that was necessary to move forward with the economic revolution. He was helped in this argument by the Cold War climate and the very useful threat of communism in general and from North Korea in particular, a threat that also required a firm hand of power and that helped to justify his political system and its use of repression.

Modernization, then, was the mission. It was the South Korean recipe for the resurrection of the Korean nation. That was a mission of such historical and national importance that it justified a government setting itself up with the power to direct the country's economic and social life single-mindedly toward the purpose it defined. South Korean authoritarianism was, in a perverse way, an idealistic form of authoritarianism.

Modernization, furthermore, was given a very specific understanding. It meant one thing and one thing only: economic development. That was, at least in the authoritarian period, what everything—power, rule, governance, business, and civic and even private life—was to be geared to. Social reform was part and parcel of the big project. Not social development instead of economic development, or even in addition to it, but social policy coordinated with economic policy so as always to be designed to contribute to economic growth.

The officers had taken control of the state. They now set about shaping that state into an instrument for their project. The purpose of that instrument was to mobilize society—the fabric of useful and/or threatening forces from below—for the project of modernization.

THE STATE

For the Korean state it could have gone either way before Park Chung Hee came to power. On the one hand, the bureaucratic system had demonstrated its ability, notably by implementing land reform in the early 1950s, no easy political or administrative task in a newly independent nation. On the other hand, corruption and favoritism had come to undermine effective governance, becoming rampant toward the last years of Rhee's presidency. The Second Republic turned into a failed democratic experiment. It was committed to economic development, but initial enthusiasm was derailed by factional infighting. The government of Prime Minister Chang was unable to assert its authority and was desperately reshuffled on a major scale three times during the nine months of its tenure. Public demonstrations and unruliness proliferated. The view took hold that Korean governments should have strong leaders.

The Presidency and the Government

President Park, building on inherited government structures, perfected a hierarchical system of bureaucratic authoritarianism in which effective decision making was confined within an institutional terrain under presidential control and from which anyone "outside" was excluded from participation.

At the top was the presidency, indeed under Park the president himself in force of both position and personal stature. The Korean state was, and has remained, strongly centralized. Until democratization, public policy was initiated, led, decided, and controlled by the president. Under the direct control of the president were the Office of the President, the "Blue House" (so named after the color of its roof tiles), and the Korean Central Intelligence Agency—the sinister KCIA, which was responsible, among various other atrocities, for the kidnapping of Kim Dae Jung in Tokyo in 1973 with the intention of dumping his body at sea had the plan not been thwarted by interventions from America, Japan, Sweden, and elsewhere.[20] The Blue House would oversee government ministries and ministerial personnel and monitor policy implementation in detail. The Central Intelligence Agency, nominally mandated to guard against North Korean infiltration, would act as an agency of surveillance over politicians (both of governing and opposition parties) as well as civil activists and government officials.

Under the Office of the President was the Economic Planning Board, which was strongly involved in policy formulation in all areas of economic policy and with extensive powers of coordination, headed by the Minister of the Economic Planning Board, who was also ex-officio the Vice Prime Minster of the government. The Ministry of Finance was the second super-ministry. The Economic Planning Board and the Ministry of Finance were designed and encouraged to compete against each other. Officials in the Economic Planning Board would play with policy ideas and long-term plans, while the Ministry of Finance would be the hard-nosed and down-to-earth executer of government policy. Other ministries were subordinate and on a lower hierarchical rung, although the ministerial balance of power would fluctuate depending on who was in charge of what and who enjoyed how much presidential confidence.

This picture of bureaucratic authoritarianism needs, however, to be qualified in at least two ways. Firstly, Park's style of exercising governance was not generally by command-and-execution. He used regular consultation meetings in which he convened senior officials from different ministries in the Blue House. The most notable were the "Monthly Meetings on Economic Trends" and the "Extended Meetings for Export Promotion." These meetings would be for presidential oversight of policy implementation, but also serve to signal policy priorities and maintain consistency of policies in the different ministries. Often the president would invite mayors of local cities, lower-ranking officials, or ordinary citizens to listen to governmental deliberations. This system of regular inter-governmental consultations was initiated by the Economic Planning Board and designed to give it presidential backing for its policy coordination and gradually became a linchpin of government operations.[21]

Secondly, it would be simplistic to see the Park regime as stable and unchanging. While the pre-1963 and post-1972 years were periods of no-nonsense hard authoritarianism, the Third Republic was mixed, neither outright democratic nor uncompromisingly authoritarian. The Constitution of the Third Republic was democratic and was approved in a referendum in December 1962. The presidential elections held during the period of the Third Republic—in 1963, 1967, and 1971—were competitive and contested. Park won the election in 1963 in a field of five candidates with 46.6 percent of the vote, against 45.1 percent for the runner-up, and in 1967 with a comfortable margin against the runner-up but still only 51.4 percent of the vote. The 1971 election was heavily manipulated by the government side, but the opposition candidate, Kim Dae Jung, nevertheless polled (officially) 45.3 percent of the vote. That experience brought to an end bureaucratic authoritarianism within a democratic shell. Park changed the constitution again and reverted to hard authoritarianism.

Advisory Agencies

The formal structure of decision making was supported by various advisory agencies that were outside of the hierarchical line of decision making but served important functions of input into it, both in the form of producing more or less specific plans and, as importantly, in introducing new ideas. These agencies were under the direction of and staffed by experts who generally saw themselves to be apolitical. The experts were dedicated to an idea of Korean advancement and of seeing Korea as a member of the community of modern nations. The government's advisors were more political than they thought and brought more than technical expertise to the project. They were animated by a vision of Korea standing proud in the modern world. They nurtured and maintained, and to some degree created, the idea of the Korean project of modernization and contributed to the fortification of that ethos by informing and stimulating the more formal structures of decision making.

In the field of social policy, the two main advisory agencies were the Committee for Social Security (CSS) and the Korea Development Institute (KDI). The CSS played an active role in social policy making in the early period of the Park government. The KDI was established in 1972 and quickly took on a major role in drafting social policy proposals in addition to those of economic policy.

In May 1962, Park ordered the cabinet to draw up a plan of social welfare programs. Strong demands for security had surfaced during the Second Republic, both from below on behalf of the low-income class and through expert opinion from above. A small and pioneering study group of social policy experts, medical doctors, and government officials had been exploring options for social policy in an informal capacity.[22] From this group, the government established a formal advisory committee as soon as Park's directive was issued, which became the CSS. This committee came up with two proposals for social policy: one for industrial accident insurance and one for health insurance. Only the recommendation

for industrial accident insurance was accepted, while the health insurance proposal was rejected as "too idealistic." Industrial accident insurance was seen to be
compatible with and supportive of economic development and was implemented
in 1964. The issue of health insurance was kicked into the log grass as an experimental pilot project for further consideration later.[23]

The KDI was established on the personal initiative of President Park to be a
center of government research on economic policy. The head of the KDI persuaded the president that a national pension program could be an effective way
to raise capital for industrialization. This was at a time when the government
embarked on a new economic strategy to promote heavy and chemical industrial
manufacturing, a strategy that would require massive capital investments. The
idea was that instead of increasing direct taxes, a national pension program
would raise capital through payroll contributions. This was the idea that was
carried forward to the 1973 National Pension Act, which was passed but immediately suspended and not revived again until 1988 under President Rho.

Throughout the 1970s, the KDI was to play the dominant role in social policy
planning while the CSS lost influence. The KDI was seen to offer safer advice on
social policy as subservient to economic development and economic policy.
Social policy for the sake of social protection was not on the agenda within the
Park government's "economy first" framework.

The National Assembly and Political Parties

The influence of the National Assembly on public policy during the Park regime
went from weak to negligible to nonexistent. Under the *Yushin* constitution,
one-third of National Assembly members were effectively appointed by the
president, and the Assembly was little more than a presidential tool.

It is true that the National Assembly often turned out to be a theater of intense
political confrontations between governing and opposition parties, with physical
confrontation more the norm than the exception. Legislation was rarely seriously
contested, opposition members seeing no reason to expend energy on matters
they could not influence and government members doing as they were told (or
answering to the KCIA). Nevertheless, political parties existed and survived and
provided institutional enclosures for competing political elites. These elites were
ready and able to come out and scramble for power on the unexpected death of
President Park in 1979. Kim Young Sam and Kim Dae Jung were the two most
prominent opposition politicians. Kim Chong-p'il, who masterminded the coup
in 1961, later joined them as a competitor for presidential power. These became
known as the "three Kims" in South Korean politics. Two of them became presidents, in 1993 and 1998, respectively, while Kim Chong-p'il failed to achieve that
ambition.

Kim Chong-p'il had organized the Democratic Republican Party soon
after the coup in 1961 to provide a political base for President Park. It was
highly organized, disciplined, and hierarchical with Park at the summit and the

other conspirators around him. Kim Chong-p'il was seen as the heir designate, but in a succession that was never to happen. Kim Dae Jung would probably have won the presidential election in 1971 had it been run honestly. Kim Young Sam led the opposition to win the general (as opposed to presidential) election in 1978.

President Park's state was authoritarian and ruthless, but not primitive. It was when necessary based on force for the preservation of power, but was surprisingly sophisticated in the way it dispensed governance. The president worked on his officials and involved them in his planning and decision making. He spoke to them, explained to them, listened to them, and created institutions for their participation. He pulled into his orbit experts and made it possible for them to work for him by allowing them the disguise of being apolitical. There was never any doubt about who was boss, but he helped his underlings to be bossed over by avoiding the humiliation of bossiness and flattering them with the pretence of cooperation.

FORCES FROM BELOW

Until democracy normalized state–society relations, the Korean polity was a pressure cooker in which forces from below either expressed their demands and complaints forcefully and at times violently, or were held down and repressed. Those forces were always there as—from the point of view of shifting governments—a difficulty with which they had to deal, frequently as a threat or perceived threat to their ability to govern.

Even during the authoritarian period after 1961, political activity was never completely denied. Interest groups were able to some degree to press their interests, business organizations often lobbied with much effect, and official trade unions pushed to advance and protect workers' interests, although with less effect. Direct political challenges came from more-or-less underground democratic and civil opposition movements, often rooted in student activism and religious groups. Despite heavy-handed oppression, civil opposition movements persistently campaigned for human rights and social justice and called for democratization. Political parties at times worked to mobilize support outside of the allowed institutional arena.

There were two powerful non-governmental structures that Park had to confront, the highly visible one of business and the less visible one of voluntarism. Neither of these did he try to crush. They were instead co-opted and bribed into roles of agency on behalf of the government. They thrived, but were skillfully eliminated as forces from below. Trade unions of organized labor were weak and fragmented; they were controlled. The rural population was left behind in the rush of industrialization; it was flattered into believing itself included. Students and other activists were militant but disorganized; they were suppressed.

The professions were poorly organized and could be ignored. An exception was the Korean Medical Association, which exerted some influence in the area of health policy, but not more for example than that it failed when it tried to block some elements (regionally differentiated pricing) of the 1977 National Health Insurance.

Capital

During the Park regime, business emerged as an influential force in policy making, although confined to working on the government's terms. Park started by purging business leaders on a blanket charge of corruption, but soon opted for cooperation with big business as the spearhead of economic growth. Most of the great *chaebŏl* were built in the 1960s from new capital and with inherited wealth entirely marginal and were the creation of the Park government's drive for economic development.[24]

The government retained a tight grip on big business by means of economic sanctions and incentives. It institutionalized inter-ministerial committees where business leaders were regular members, with meetings often chaired by Park himself. If businesses accepted the government's leadership and met export and other targets, there followed capital subsidies in the form of low-interest loans and tax relief. The government controlled licenses to operate in strategic sectors such as the motor and heavy and chemical industries, which virtually guaranteed the winner of a license monopoly status. Indifference to the government's line would put businesses in serious risk. Since the banks were mostly controlled by the government, it could pull the plug on credit at will. In social policy, business was a reluctant partner forced to bear the cost of emerging social insurance. Employers were, to put it carefully, not enthusiastic about social protection but were perforce careful not to oppose government policy. Instead, they tried to exercise influence in the guise of technical advice on matters such as the way of settling compensation disputes arising from industrial accidents, or indirectly via think tanks, such as the Centre for Korean Economic Studies, which was set up by the Korean Chamber of Commerce and Industry as a voice for restraint and incrementalism in social policy.

Labor

After the coup in 1961, the government ordered trade unions to reorganize. Leaders were purged. Local trade unions at the firm level were prohibited, and only unions based on industrial sectors were allowed. The Federation of the Korean Trade Unions was set up based on national industrial sector unions, the number of which reached 16 by 1963.

The government dealt with unions through a combination of control and co-optation. Union leaders were under constant surveillance but were also bought off by being pulled into government circles, for instance as members of the National Assembly or to senior positions in government ministries.

The FKTU was unable to represent workers' interests effectively or to do much to advance workers' rights. Union leaders were bogged down in factional infighting and generally more geared toward exploiting government largess than engaging in union activity proper.

In the early 1970s, labor pressure began to increase partly as a result of a reduced influx of new labor from rural areas and partly because of persistently harsh working conditions.[25] A textile worker, Chŏn T'ae-il, who set fire to himself as a protest against working conditions in the textile industry on November 11, 1970, became a symbol of labor exploitation. Tension increased on university campuses and in many workplaces. The government responded in December 1971 with a Special Decree for National Security, according to which it could ban any union activity in industries that it defined as critical for economic development or national security.

Working conditions deteriorated further by the opportunistic behavior of many employers. As oil prices went up and the rate of industry profit fell, employers turned to squeezing the cost of labor and engaging in rampantly unfair practices, such as layoffs without due process and late payment of wages. Government efforts to contain unfair and illegal working practices were to little avail. Union membership stood at no more than 10 to 20 percent of the industrial workforce throughout the 1970s. The government itself resorted to illegal measures of control, such as drawing up "blacklists" of workers who had been involved in organizing what were called "democratic trade unions," which were secretly distributed to employers to keep union activists out of the workforce.

In 1979, female workers of the YH Trade Textile Company staged a sit-in protest in the office of the opposition party to protest against their working conditions and to demand unpaid wages. Kim Young Sam, then the leader of the party, supported the workers. This enraged President Park, who ordered the governing party to dismiss Kim from the National Assembly. That provoked popular unrest in Pusan, the second-largest city in Korea and Kim's political home, which in turn spilled over to the neighboring Masan area. Workers in Special Export Zones in these areas joined in the protest. As the unrest spread, the police were unable to control the situation, and the threat of labor revolt became a serious political issue. The government fell into disarray. Top security officials were unable to agree on to how to respond and advised the president in different directions. The meeting after which President Park was killed in October 1979 was convened to find a solution to the Pusan and Masan protest. In a quagmire of uprisings from below and paralysis from above, the Park regime came to a sudden and unexpected end.

The Rural Constituency

Industrialism brought decline to rural areas, which were depleted by providing workers to rapidly developing urban industries. Out of this decline emerged what became known as the *Saemaul* Movement, the New Community Movement.

This movement was to provide, on the one hand, a response to social needs in the countryside and, on the other hand, an ideological message of self-reliance that became strongly influential in rural populations and spilled over into industrial organization in the Factory *Saemaul* Movement (more on this in Chapter 3). Much of the population was pulled into what became in effect a cultural revolution, and, what is remarkable, a successful one.

The movement was launched as a government initiative in 1970 and grew out of the example of a village in the Southeast province of *Kyŏngbuk*, where farmers had mobilized resources and labor to improve village infrastructure. Capitalizing on a success story, the government provided a small amount of subsidy and moved on to replicate the experience in other rural villages.[26]

President Park visited the village and spoke to local people and officials about the force of self-help, self-reliance, and cooperation. The government distributed 300 packs of cement to each of 35,000 villages, which they could use for community projects of their own choice. Roads were repaired, bridges built, sanitation improved, homes renovated, community halls raised, co-operatives established. Certainly, those packs of cement were only a small part of what was necessary for the development projects, but they enabled village people to contribute their own labor and mobilize other resources. From a base of less than 400 pilot projects in 1971, the movement grew to between two and three thousand projects in 1978.[27]

There were material consequences. Rural people acquired resources, and projects could be undertaken and facilitated. It made some contribution to filling the gap in living standards between urban and rural populations. It made Korea's project of economic development more broad-based than it might have been. It contributed to the modernization of rural and farming populations.

At the same time it was a project of political mobilization and yet another effort in the government's purchase of legitimacy. Although participation was voluntary, broad, and enthusiastic, it was still a state-orchestrated program to marshal support for an authoritarian regime. It coincided with Park's manipulation of the constitution first by enabling him to stand for president for a third time in 1971 and then reverting to hard authoritarianism in 1972. It brought a message of self-reliance to poor people from an all-powerful government. It enabled the same government to extend the message and experience of voluntarism and self-help to an oppressed industrial labor force, and from there to divert energy and attention away from unionization, wage demands, and workers' rights to self-help and voluntary project work.

THE WELFARE STATE

The Korean welfare state has evolved gradually as the arch-typical case of the developmental welfare regime, on a path similar to that of other East Asian "tigers" such as Taiwan, Hong Kong, Singapore, Malaysia, and, in an earlier trajectory, Japan. This represents a distinct welfare state model, as compared to the various European and related regimes. In the developmental welfare state, social policy is intimately linked with and subordinate to the supreme goal of economic development. Regulation is the main policy instrument, and government social spending is kept to a low level. It differs from European models in that state provision of social security and services plays a marginal role.[28]

Within this model, a division emerged after 1997 and in response to the Asian economic crisis. Korea in particular, but also Taiwan, responded to the crisis with reforms that made the welfare state more inclusive, while the welfare states of Hong Kong, Singapore, and (largely) Malaysia remained more unchangingly selective.[29] The explanation of Korean deviation from developmental orthodoxy is that the economic crisis coincided with democratic consolidation in a way that coalesced into a new social contract between forces from below and above (more on this in Chapter 5).

The state broadened its responsibilities for unemployment compensation and social assistance. Statutory social protection had previously been available to selected and relatively privileged groups, mainly public employees and core industrial workers, while vulnerable sections of the population were left outside of the system. Now, new policies reached out to hitherto marginalized groups. In the process, the state moved from being mainly a regulator of protection to making itself more of a provider. The Korean welfare state was thus taken some way in the direction of a European model. It has remained predominantly a welfare state based on the politics of regulation but now with a stronger component of state provision.[30] A chronology of welfare state development in Korea is given in Table 2.

Social Insurance

Welfare states typically consist of arrangements of social assistance, social security, and social services. The state either regulates for others to make provisions or takes on provision responsibilities itself.

The seeds of social security were sown in early and carefully selective legislation: the Military and Police Assistance Acts of 1950 and 1951, the Civil Servant Pension Acts of 1960 and 1963, the Military Personnel Pension Act of 1963, and the Private School Teachers Pension Act of 1973. This legislation was designed to give protection and security to select groups of mainly public-sector workers who were seen to be strategically important for the government, and was never a means to protect vulnerable groups in society. In 1962, the Park government dramatically improved the civil service pension by awarding pension rights after twenty years of service and irrespective of age, in an undisguised ploy to buy loyalty from its own servants. Civil servants were not well paid compared to counterparts in the private sector, but they did have job security and were now given the promise of privileged pensions in the future.

Table 2: The Development of the Welfare State With Key Features

Period	Prevailing Ideology	Range of Social Commitments	Major legislation		
			Social assistance	Social insurance	Social services
Tentative democracy (First & Second Republics, 1948–60)	Pauperism	Marginalized	Military Relief Act (1950) Police Relief Act (1951)	Civil Service Pension Act (1960)	Regulations on Charity Donations (1951)
Hard authoritarianism (Military Junta, 1961–63)	The developmental welfare state	Selective social insurance Residual social assistance Quasi-government agencies mobilized	Livelihood Protection Act (1961)	Military Personnel National Pension (1963) Industrial Accident Insurance Act (1963) National Health Insurance Act (1963, implemented 1977	Child Welfare Act (1961) Foreign Relief Agencies Act (1963)
Soft authoritarianism (Third Republic, 1963–72)				Civil Service Pension Act, revised (1963)	Social Welfare Service Act (1970)
Hard authoritarianism (Fourth & Fifth Republics, 1972–87)			Livelihood Protection Act revised (1983) Minimum Wage Act (1986, implemented 1988)	National Pension Act (1973, revised 1986, implemented 1988) Private School Teachers Pension Act (1973) National Health Insurance revised (1977, 1979, 1981, 1986, 1987) Civil Servant Pensions revised (1982, 1983)	Social Welfare Service Fund Act (1980) Elderly Welfare Act (1981) Handicapped Welfare Act (1981) Child Welfare Act revised (1981)

(continued)

Table 2: The Development of the Welfare State With Key Features (*cont.*)

Period	Prevailing Ideology	Range of Social Commitments	Major legislation		
			Social assistance	Social insurance	Social services
Re-democratization (Sixth Republic, 1987–98)	Welfare Expansion under Globalism	Comprehensive social insurance Minor expansion of social assistance	Basic Law for Social Security (1995) Livelihood Protection Act revised (1991)	Employment Insurance Act (1993, implemented 1995) National Pension Act revised (1995) National Health Insurance Act revised (1989, 1991, 1994, 1995)	Community Chest Law (1997) Child Welfare Act revised (1989, 1997) Elderly Welfare Act revised (1993, 1997) Social Welfare Service Act revised (1997)
Democratic consolidation (Sixth Republic, 1998–)	Productive Welfare	Substantial reforms of social assistance Service provision by voluntary agencies under state–society partnership	National Basic Livelihood Security Act (1999)	Unemployment Insurance extended (1998) National Pension Act revised (1998, 1999, 2008) Civil Service Pension Act revised (2009)	Nonprofit and Voluntary Organisations Assistance Act (2000) Community Chest Law revised (1999, 2001, 2002)

Gradually, social security would be broadened beyond the public sector, but again in a selective way. Typically, workers in large enterprises—strategic workers again—would be awarded some protection that would not extend to workers in the more marginal reaches of the economy. Only with democratic consolidation would the welfare state break away from selectivity. Fragmented health insurance was restructured to widen risk pooling in favor of people who were more risk-prone and less well-off. The safety net of state social assistance was extended to people who had hitherto been considered to be outside of its responsibility: the working poor, the elderly with working-age children (who would previously carry the duty of care), the able-bodied unemployed, and the self-employed.

Social security was from the beginning organized as social insurance, and that has persisted. The state has regulated for others to provide, with funding coming from insurance contributions. It has not and does not fund social insurance out of taxation, except obviously in its role as an employer. Some public money would typically be provided on the introduction of social insurance programs to cover administrative costs and build up administrative structures, but once administrations were up and running as quasi-public agencies, the programs would typically operate without government subvention (although for the industrial accident insurance, for example, a small administrative subsidy was re-introduced in 1978, having been discontinued after the program's first two years).

Far from paying for social security, the government initially saw social insurance as a source of funding for other purposes. The first attempt toward a national pension system, in 1973, was premised on an idea that contributory pensions could be a way of mobilizing capital for industrial investment. That attempt, however, failed for other reasons, and when national pensions were revived in 1986, the alchemic idea that investment capital would grow out of pensions was no longer salient.

The first step toward inclusiveness in social insurance was taken with the introduction of industrial accident insurance in 1963, in conjunction with the ambitious if formalistic Five-Year Economic Development Plan. This—the extending of social security to industrial workers and beyond the narrow circle of public employees—marked the first qualitative leap of discontinuity in the development of the Korean welfare state. The insurance was introduced in workplaces with 500 employees or more and has since been gradually extended so that by 2005 four out of ten persons in the workforce were covered, those remaining outside of coverage being irregular workers, farmers, and other self-employed.

This was not the beginning of social policy, but it was the first step toward a modern welfare state. That, then, was an initiative of the military dictatorship. President Park was from the start of his reign aware that he needed a social dimension to give his rule legitimacy. It was clear that if social reforms were to pay off for him, they had to come from him and be seen as part of what his rule would involve. He had to visibly make himself a social reformer.

However, with the unequivocal priority of economic growth, a priority that involved maximum economic support for business, there was not much room for spending or the use of administrative resources for soft social concerns. Social reforms could and should be initiated by the state, which is to say by the president, but they would mainly have to be paid for from elsewhere and delivered by others. The solution was, firstly, to build up social security on the basis of insurance, and secondly, less noticeably, to build on the tradition of voluntary agencies for the delivery of social services. Thus was set in motion the development of the peculiar Korean welfare state: on the one hand the building of an unequivocally strong state and on the other the allowing of that state to become dependent on non-state actors for the delivery of important components of its governance. The president was able to show initiative and make decisions but unloaded funding to insurance premiums paid for by employers and workers and the burden of service delivery to non-government agencies.

After industrial accident insurance followed in order the other standard components of social insurance: health, pensions, and unemployment. Even inclusive social insurance would be introduced selectively, typically starting, strategically again, in firms with more than 500 employees and being extended gradually to embrace a larger section of the workforce. Extensions in social insurance would at times be given from above to fend off pressures on authoritarian governments and at times come as spoils of democratic struggles from below.

Health insurance was introduced as a limited experimental pilot program in 1965 and made compulsory for selected categories of workers in the public sector, schools, and large enterprises in 1977. Some smaller enterprises could join on a voluntary basis. In 1978, government employees and private school teachers became compulsory members and, as of 1981, the self-employed could join. By 1987, most employees in manufacturing industries had access to health insurance. Throughout the 1980s, coverage increased rapidly and reached about 90 percent of the population. Until then, health insurance had been a middle class privilege of great practical and symbolic value. Through National Health Insurance reforms in 1998, 1999, 2000, and 2002, more than 300 health funds were pooled into a national system extending coverage in principle to the whole population.

There is a mixed ownership of health care institutions. Most hospitals and clinics have been and are run by nonprofit foundations, with a minority of national hospitals run by the state and provincial hospitals by local governments. Small-scale clinics (less than 100 beds) can be established and run by individual practitioners. Health insurance typically covers most but not all treatments, at prices decided by the Ministry of Health and Social Welfare, and excluding a patient fee of typically 20 (inpatient treatment) to 30 (outpatient treatment) percent of the cost.

A National Pension Act was passed in 1973 but immediately shelved due to the effects of the oil price crisis of the same year, and did not resurface for implementation until 1988. By 1994, 27 percent of the working population was covered. In 1999, the program was extended to farmers and other self-employed and short-term contract workers on a voluntary basis. Full pensions were first paid from 2008 (due to a 20-year contribution requirement). The average full pension was then at about 90 percent of the poverty line for a two-person household and about 150 percent of the single-person poverty line. An elderly couple would hence hardly be able to live on the pension if the husband, as was usual, had been the single breadwinner. By 2009, about 2.2 million persons were in receipt of the full pension. The Korean labor market has been divided between a core sector of regular employment in public services and big business and a large fringe of irregular work and self-employment. Social security coverage has consistently lagged in the irregular labor market, something that is reflected presently in, for example, strongly stratified retirement between previously regular and irregular workers. That stratification sticks deep, not only to standards of living but also to welfare and social integration more broadly.[31]

Unemployment compensation was introduced in 1993 as part of the Employment Insurance Act. Also included in the act were training and job security provisions in the form of subventions to job training institutions, which may be private or public, and to employers for retaining workers. As of 1998, access to unemployment compensation was radically extended.

The most recently introduced social insurance, as of 2008, is for long-term care, administered as part of the National Health Insurance. Service providers are mostly private and operate on a fee-for-service basis.

Occupational Welfare
In the core field of social insurance, the Korean welfare state was built as a system of occupational welfare and of state-enforced cooperation between employers and employees. That was to be an uneasy cooperation, involving reactionary employers, ruthless big business, workers who oscillated between militancy and docility, and unions that would at times take on the employers and the state and at times mostly fight each other.

Occupational welfare did not originate in social insurance but in earlier legislation on working conditions and workers' rights. The Labor Standard Act was passed in 1953 as part of a package of legislation on industrial relations that was remarkably progressive for its time. This legislation would in long periods be poorly implemented and of no more than feeble effectiveness, but it did establish a standard around which worker and union militancy could be and was mobilized.

Social Services

The provision of social services was brought to Korea by foreign, mainly American, voluntary agencies after independence and in particular after the end of the Korean War. That established a tradition of non-state agency for the provision of services that persists to this day. Here, as with social security, the state has been and continues to be regulator more than provider.

The field would gradually be taken over by Korean agencies as foreign voluntarism was wound down. Often, the heavy hand of state regulation was such that technically autonomous agencies were in reality quasi-governmental institutions. However, and remarkably, even during the harshest periods of dictatorship, civil society agencies were allowed and encouraged to operate outside of the apparatus of the state.

State provision has been marginal in the Korean welfare state, but not absent. Some personal social services, such as home care, are provided by local government, with partial subvention from the state. These services have been narrowly targeted to low-income families and have been of very limited reach. Since the introduction of autonomous local government and democratic consolidation, there has been relentless pressure on local governments to increase their provision of personal services to the needy. One innovation in the field is a (so far limited) introduction of vouchers that enable clients to make use of providers of their own choice.

Social Assistance

The Korean welfare state, as generally elsewhere, grew from a base of poor relief as a continuous state provision. This was a colonial legacy. Poor relief had been brought under legislative order in the *Chosŏn* Poor Law of 1944, which provided for state support to certain categories of the elderly, the disabled, pregnant women, and children. This continued under various decrees of the American Military Government and during the First Republic, including in new provisions of targeted relief for military and police personnel. The Livelihood Protection Act of 1961 (revised in 1983, 1991, and 1997) improved the system of poor relief but did not mark a shift in the character of relief. That was to happen only with the National Basic Livelihood Security Act of 1999, which abolished poor relief in its old form and brought in a new model of social assistance.

Here we are at the second leap of discontinuity in the development of the Korean welfare state, discontinuity in the sense that something qualitatively new was introduced. From 1998, unemployment compensation was improved and extended. The state thereby took on radically new duties of provision. Then, in 1999, conventional and discretionary poor relief was thrown out and replaced with a modern rights-based system of social assistance. Although the state had long been a provider of poor relief, provision had been entirely marginal and of little or no real consequence for the alleviation of poverty, and care for the poor had in practical terms been a family responsibility. With the new act in 1999, the state in principle took on the responsibility of a guaranteed social minimum and for the associated provision.

The transformation was far from monumental in quantitative terms. The social safety net remained incomplete and with big holes. Public spending on social welfare, including social assistance, edged upward but remains on a decidedly low level in comparison to other OECD countries. The social security budget was, in 2003, for example, still at less than 2 percent of GDP and less than 10 percent of the total government budget. But it did represent a qualitative shift with significant consequences not only in social policy but also in governance more generally. The established welfare state structure was one of state regulation of provisions via businesses and voluntary agencies. Now, cautiously, a third pillar was being built of state provision. That presented the state with a new welfare partner, that of local government, now reconstituted on the basis of local autonomy. State provision of social assistance could be decided centrally but would perforce have to be delivered through local authorities. While the state's coalitions with business and voluntarism had been polished and made to run smoothly, the new experience of state provision via more-or-less autonomous local administrations landed the government with an unexpected problem of having to implement its own policies. It found itself in control of decision making but not of implementation.

STRONG STATE AND MIXED GOVERNANCE

Did it work? Did social reform help the Park regime to hold on to power? Did it contribute to effective governance and to economic advancement and modernization more broadly?

Park himself lasted nearly twenty years, and would have lasted longer had he lived. The authoritarian regime went on for eight more years, and the conservative elite it had created clung on for another ten years. Modernization followed and was by and large delivered in the form the state had defined. The economy grew ferociously. Standards of living improved—the rate of absolute poverty, for example, was brought down from 40 percent of all households in 1965 to 10 percent by 1980, and steadily further down after that.[32] Working conditions improved, and the rate of industrial accidents (victims relative to 1,000 workers) fell from 5.9 in 1965 to 3.0 in 1980.

Pre-democracy governments were brutal and unrestrained in the means they used to take and hold on to power, but prudently effective in governance. One memory of South Korea in the 1970s and 1980s is of constant unruliness with student activism and riots met by police brutality. Of this there was much.

It was also significant, not as a serious threat, except at critical junctures, but as a constant reminder of democratic pressure in the form of pinpricks from below into the backsides of the rulers above. But, appearances notwithstanding, the result was not a divided country. Rather, the nation *was* mobilized for the modernization project. Capital was mobilized. It was rewarded handsomely, but on the condition of compliance. Labor was mobilized. It never ceased to make trouble and to be coerced in return, but it delivered the goods in hard work. The rural population was mobilized in the aftermath of land reform by being made to feel not neglected. Voluntary agencies were mobilized by being allowed to operate in return for staying apolitical. Government officials and advisors were mobilized by being listened to and made partners in governance. There was nothing soft in the use and display of power by this state, but in governance power was used smartly and with some restraint.[33] Park's strategy was to co-opt broadly and to pull into the government's orbit, by a combination of force, trickery, and integration, anyone he could make use of and who could otherwise make trouble for him. There is a paradox here: all-powerful rulers who governed as much by mobilizing as by commanding, or possibly more by mobilizing than by commanding.

The direct effects of social policies during the Park years were not much to speak of. His initiatives were symbolically significant, but material implementation was thin on the ground. The industrial accident insurance might have had some impact on economic development. This came early and started to remove uncertainty for both employers and workers and may have contributed to bringing down the rate of industrial accidents. Civil service, military, and teacher pensions may have stimulated public sector morale, although they were distributed regressively by benefitting mainly people in the middle of the income distribution. Social assistance was too tight and strictly means-tested to have any impact on the overall distribution of income or poverty rates. National Health Insurance started to get off the ground at the end of Park's tenure, but too late to produce results that he could cash in on, and was again geared predominantly to relatively better-off workers in large firms.

Even so, although dictatorial and often brutal, including in the repression of workers and unions, the regime was not socially unresponsive. It forced employers to be at least marginally better employers than they were inclined to be, for example by enforcing occupational welfare and training measures. It responded to rural despair. It encouraged and enabled voluntary agencies to engage in social work. It launched social insurance and held up the promise of steadily better social security in the future. It released benevolent, if manipulative, mass mobilization in the name of community and self-reliance.

The revolution Park had articulated in 1963 happened. It came at a heavy price of freedom and civil rights denied and periods of rampant state brutality against opposition forces, but it did happen. It was a revolution led by the state he created. Social reform was integrated into the fabric of that state. The causal contribution of social initiatives to modernization is difficult to establish and measure, but there was a system at work in which the social dimension was indispensible. That system was more compromising than it might have been and more than Park had the power to make it. When we look beyond power and follow through to governance, we see a system that was less monolithic than it appears on first sight. A modus of working was established in which the state ruled with and through non-state actors that it courted and cultivated. It was clearly a strong state, but in the nitty-gritty of how it worked, it was also one of mixed governance.

3

THE STATE MEETS BUSINESS

The welfare state as an instrument of rule came to Korea on the back of authoritarian government. The dictators needed to be seen to respond to demands in
the population, but also to do so without imposing a new burden of expenditure
on state budgets. Their priority was economic development, and what they
had of budget capacity they were determined to direct toward investments. The
solution in social security was the politics of regulation and occupational
welfare. The government would legislate for social security and shift the burden
of payment and delivery on to business. To make this work, it had to mobilize
capital and neutralize labor.

The relationship between state, capital, and labor has been continuously fluctuating and was never simple or easy. The government side would move from
bribing businesses with direct or tax subsidies to the arrest of businessmen and
the confiscation of property. Businesses would obediently follow government
leadership, but also maneuver with bribery of their own of officials and politicians and whatever they could get away with of tax evasion and avoidance. Labor
would in periods unionize and engage in industrial action and militancy and in
other periods be held down by repression, but also often be betrayed from within
by corrupt union leadership. Occupational welfare was one of shifting governments' instruments for forging order out of the continuous threat of industrial
chaos.

ECONOMIC DEVELOPMENT

By the end of the century, Korea ranked eleventh among industrial countries by size of the economy. In the 1980s and '90s, the economy grew by 7 to 12 percent per year. In the 1980s alone, the value of the stock market increased 28-fold.[34] The South Korean population grew from 19 million in 1950 to 47 million at the turn of the century (a growth that is expected to turn to decline from a probable peak of 49 million in about 10 years' time, due to now ultra-low fertility).

It started in a pitiful state. At the end of the Korean War, about two-thirds of the working population were in farming, but agricultural production was still not enough to feed the nation. Industrialization had been introduced during the colonial period, but only as a foretaste. Manufacturing accounted for less than 10 percent of output.[35] There was a lack of investment and few sources of capital except foreign aid. Although the economy grew steadily during the 1950s, this was mitigated by inflation and population pressure. The influx of 1.8 million North Koreans during the war contributed to a shortage of consumer goods and housing. Disproportionate resources were absorbed in a bloated and coercive state apparatus. In the Cold War climate, the Rhee government was able to extract a steady flow of aid from the United States and was not actively pursuing any policy of systematic industrialization. As a result, the Korean economy remained strongly aid-dependent throughout Syngman Rhee's reign.[36]

Industrialization was nevertheless progressing. Population was gravitating to towns and cities from the countryside, and from agriculture to manufacturing. Land reform, the great legacy of the Rhee years to Korea's economic development, had wiped out land-based capital and cleared space for a new breed of entrepreneurial capitalists. The economic climate was corrupt. Profiteers benefited from U.S. aid and from government contacts. The symbiotic, if often uneasy, relationship between government and big business was in the making. Huge holdings of wealth were accumulating on private hands. Just when the structure of the Korean economy matured into one dominated by the conglomerates that came to be known as *chaebŏl* is not easily said, but this economy was clearly in gestation.

At the end of the First and during the short Second Republic, economic planning started to come into more systematic forms. Economic development plans were drawn up, premised on additional U.S. support and with a strong emphasis on public works and infrastructural investments.[37]

The coup d'état in 1961 strengthened the message of economic development as a national ambition. The junta published its first Five-Year Economic Plan after only two months, drawing on the planning work of the previous government. The plan aimed to advance industrial development and to transform the industrial structure from labor intensive and elementary technologies toward import-substitution based on relatively sophisticated manufacturing of intermediate products, consumer durables, and machinery.

This plan demanded enormous financial inputs, for which foreign resource became the main source. The government turned to underwriting the foreign borrowing of private firms. It thereby became closely involved with private business and used its leverage, and the threat of withdrawing it, to make business increasingly government dependent. The collusion of government and big business in the project of industrialization was taking shape.

During the 1960s, an excess of production capacity and the saturation of domestic markets pushed companies toward foreign markets. The government changed its policy from import-substitution to stimulating exports. Exporting companies found themselves benefiting from easy access to foreign loans, subsidized credit, tax exemptions, and import and other forms of protectionism. The direction of industrial policy had changed, but not the instruments: the strong intervention of the government in business life and the heavy dependence and subordination of big business to government.

Between 1965 and 1973, the economy grew at an average annual GNP rate of 10 percent and maintained relative price stability. Both employment and labor productivity increased strongly. The period has not surprisingly been characterized as a "golden age" for Korea's economy.[38]

With the *Yushin* constitution in 1972, President Park took extraordinary powers. He redesigned economic policy again, making the promotion of heavy and chemical industries the centerpiece of industrial development, and strengthened even more the involvement of government in detailed business decisions. Prioritized firms were designated and selected for support with credit, tax subsidies, guarantees, protective licensing and regulations, and other measures. Large companies that were seen to have the capacity to take on new production responsibilities were singled out for support. President Park was directly involved, personally meeting with business leaders, on the one hand pressuring them to toe the government line and, on the other hand, typically issuing orders to ministers to help designated companies to solve financial and other problems.[39]

The economy responded with another burst of growth. From 1970 to 1978, the average annual growth rate of the manufacturing sector reached almost 20 percent and of the heavy and chemical industries specifically about 30 percent.[40] Employment in the manufacturing sector increased from 13 percent of total employment in 1970 to 23 percent in 1979, by which time employment in heavy and chemical industries accounted for more than half of total employment in manufacturing.[41] The dark side of this push for growth was the burden of foreign debt. By the late 1970s, the Korean economy showed serious signs of overheating, with export performance deteriorating and inflation reaching a level near 20 percent in 1979.[42]

Upon seizing office in May 1980, General Chun and his economic advisors had to deal with a combination of high inflation, sluggish growth, and rising unemployment. To overcome recession, and at the cost of rising budget deficits, the government increased public works, reduced taxes, lowered interest rates, and devalued the currency, the *won*. Other tax and credit measures aimed to reduce the financial burden on companies.

By the end of 1982, the economy was showing signs of recovery with, for example, rising exports in heavy machinery and shipbuilding. The government, however, moved to stabilization policies due to, again, the increasing burden of foreign debt. In April 1984, it issued a revised version of the Five-Year Plan for the years 1981 to 1986, with price stabilization as the overarching goal. It froze the state budget for 1984, reduced credit growth to the private sector, eliminated most interest-rate subsidies to heavy and chemical industries, froze public sector wages for the year and limited their rate of growth to below 5 percent until 1987, and used state banks as agents to control wage increases in private companies.

By late 1984, the economy was in recovery and the government again expanded export credits and increased the availability of credit to small and medium-sized companies. This coincided with lower oil prices and lower international interest rates. The Korean export sector responded quickly, and exports increased by 28 percent in 1986.

With the Roh government, Korea left autocracy behind and turned hesitantly back to democracy. The new government was cautiously expansionist in economic policy, increasing public spending and private access to credit. While exports increased and the economy was generally in good shape, the downside was now a rapidly rising cost of labor. With democratization, the government operated in a new political setting. It was dependent on the National Assembly but was not in command of a working majority. A series of demonstrations organized by militant trade unions in 1987 and 1988 resulted in high wage increases.[43]

However, in spite of the rising cost of labor, the massive investment associated with the 1988 Seoul Olympics, increased exports, and a strong currency all contributed to rapid economic growth. From 1988 to 1992, growth reached 8.3 percent on average. There were, however, strong underlying inflationary pressures. A seriously contributing factor was the rising price of housing. Although the government launched an ambitious program of (low-cost) house building, housing market inflation would not subside.[44]

The formation of a broad conservative political coalition in 1990 gave the government firmer control over economic policy. New stimuli were announced, including devaluation, credit easing, and a lowering of interest rates. Fiscal policy became more expansionist as the elections of 1991 and 1992 approached.

President Kim Young Sam initiated an economic recovery package under the label of "New Economic Policy," composed of interest rate cuts and increased supply of facility investment funds. The great concern now became the effects of economic globalization and the maintenance of international competitiveness under the pressure of higher labor costs. The response was deregulation in financial and labor markets. That introduced "flexibility" as a theme that was to bedevil industrial relations for a decade until labor market reforms could be settled by

President Kim Dae Jung. The economy had then taken a nosedive as a result of the Asian economic crisis in 1997, and economic policy had been put temporarily under the administration of the International Monetary Fund.

From 2000, the economy slowly recovered and climbed back into stable economic growth, but as a different and more market-sensitive system. The price of flexibility was an increasing number of non-regular or temporary workers and higher rates of unemployment, particularly among the young.

During the period from roughly 1950 to 2000, the Korean economy was in steady and strong growth, albeit first hesitantly and later with temporary setbacks. Economic policy falls into three rough sub-periods. The First Republic can be seen as a scramble for some element of political order toward the new experience of industrial capitalism. During the authoritarian period from 1961 to 1987, order was imposed from above in the form of government-controlled industrial development, in a policy that was remarkably successful in terms of economic growth. That gave way to a gradual winding back of government control, first tentatively and hesitantly in the last years of authoritarian rule and then with gradually more determination during re-democratization. The developmental state that first crowded out tentative democracy was itself dismantled in favor of democratic normality.

CAPITAL

Industrial capitalism established itself during the 1950s under the influence of economic aid from the American and Korean governments. Entrepreneurial success was a matter of exploiting aid and depended more on government connections than on productivity. Thus was born the business–government coalition that was to characterize, if in shifting ways, the Korean economy until, and to some degree into, the period of democratization.

General Park first justified the 1961 coup by assigning two main tasks to the new regime: the removal of corrupt business–government relations and the alleviation of poverty. To him, Korean society had been made unruly by corruption, and poverty was a result of an associated lack of discipline and social order. Politicians, businessmen, and hooligans who had profiteered during the Syngman Rhee years were to be purged to clear the way for new economic and social relations that would be orderly, transparent, and efficient.[45]

This resulted initially in both confiscatory policies and the arrest of businessmen for illicit wealth accumulation. The display of power by the junta and its clear will to use it caused business to align itself with the new regime and to propose a deal, which General Park accepted, to substitute economic fines for criminal prosecutions.[46] That deal was accepted by Park because his developmental zeal was stronger than his antipathy against the old regime. He accepted, against his own instinct, that there would be no development without the participation and contribution of business and capital, however reprehensible. Hence, the business–government coalition, against which the coup had in part been directed, survived, albeit on new terms dictated by the government side.

The deal with the government led big business to start organizing. A group of entrepreneurs, including some released from prison, set up the Association of Korean Industries in August 1961. The purpose was partly to stimulate the enterprise that was urgently needed to pay the fines that businesses had been forced to accept and partly to convey a common cause with the dictatorship. In 1968, the AKI was reconstituted as a more broadly based business association in the Federation of Korean Industries. Over the years, shifting governments maintained close links with business through these and other associations in the formulation of economic policy. The government would press business to work according to its developmental plans, and business would extract beneficial concessions from the government. In addition to organization, business would use bribery, political contributions, and occasionally collective action to convey its message to the political masters. The government established both formal and informal networks with the business community to advance its own policies, but the government–business relationship was never wholly authoritarian or top-down. There were continuous consultations, negotiations, and compromises between the two sides.

The industrial policy of the Park government was one of choice and concentration: the government chose the industries to be promoted and concentrated resources on one or a few companies within each industry. Winning in this closed consultation required compliance with the government's industrial strategy, capacity to implement projects and prepare new ones, and unscrupulous skills of maneuvering within authoritarian and corrupt politics. In the resulting large corporations, the *chaebŏl*, ownership and power was under the control of new capital and typically concentrated in the hands of the founder or the founder's family and selected managers.[47]

Although industrial policy was heavily focused on a small number of large corporations, the economy was made up of predominantly small and medium-sized businesses. The dual structure—with the large *chaebŏl* on the one side controlling the majority of industrial capital, and the many smaller businesses on the other side employing the majority of industrial workers—has been a characteristic of the Korean economy. When the welfare state started to reach beyond public-sector workers, that was predominantly within the *chaebŏl* economy, and the secondary economy was by and large unaffected until much later.

The rapid growth of big business, guided and supported by the government, created an industrial structure in which small and medium-sized companies made themselves suppliers and in that way subservient to the big domestic exporters. As manufacturing transformed from light to heavy industry, the quality and productivity of the small and medium-sized companies, which supplied inputs to the exporting corporations, became a serious concern.

These companies were a significant arena of industrial relations dispute in the period since most industrial confrontations and labor organizations were located in smaller companies. The Act for the Promotion of Small and Medium-Sized Companies in 1978 and the establishment in 1979 of a quasi-governmental organization, the Small and Medium Business Corporation, were part of a policy to promote technology and productivity in small and medium companies.

The "labor issue" was consistently a major concern for business in its dealings with the government, the tenor of which is illustrated by a submission in February 1965 from the Korean Chamber of Commerce and Industry, entitled "A Policy Proposal for the Economy," with demands to restrict trade union activity and reduce the scope of occupational welfare.[48] It proposed that trade unionism should be directed away from an industry-based and toward an enterprise-based system in order to prevent any pressure or interference from industry-based unions in collective bargaining at enterprise level. The size of companies subject to the Labor Standards Act should be increased from 30 to more than 50 employees. Prosecution should not be brought against employers for any violation of the Labor Standards Act. The government should intervene in industrial disputes, in particular in export companies. Paid maternity leave should be reduced from 60 to 40 days. Restrictions on overtime should be changed from 60 to 72 hours per week, and the overtime payment rate should be reduced from 50 percent to 25 percent. Paid menstruation leave, which allowed female workers to have one day of paid leave per month, should be abolished. In the face of increasing labor pressure from below, employers continued to press for restrictions from above and continued to improve their organization. The Korean Employers Federation was established in 1970 to deal specifically with labor issues.

The decisive crackdown on union activism came with the return of hard authoritarianism when President Park seized almost unlimited power to restrict civil liberties and control wages and prices, under the guise of "national security." From 1972, collective bargaining and all other collective action were practically banned.

With the Chun regime (as of 1980), the developmental alliance between government and business started to change shape again. The overpowering personal influence of President Park was in the past and the economy in turmoil. Stabilization policies in response to the symptoms of stagflation left big business feeling exposed compared to its protected status during the expansionary policies of previous governments. The new government, having established itself through a coup, needed to mark its distance from the previous regime and found it opportune to blame the chaebŏl and the system of state-led heavy industry for the economic troubles.

Careful liberalizations with the stabilization policies were exploited by business to push for more consistent liberalizations, including in financial markets. As inflation was gradually pushed back, the government again lowered interest rates. The economy was in recovery, making business less dependent on the government. The price of oil fell. The value of the U.S. dollar relative to the Japanese *yen* dropped dramatically. Lower global interest rates improved the financial situation of Korean companies, most of which were carrying large debts. Korean companies improved their export competitiveness, especially against Japan. The market was allowed to work more freely, and the selection system was relaxed. The developmental state began to be gradually dismantled.

The government introduced financial sector reforms in the interest of making credit fairer and less preferential to big businesses, but with the unintended consequence of weakening its own capacity to control business.[49] Although the intention was to reduce the advantages of companies favored by the government, which were mostly large *chaebŏl*, the reform opened up new opportunities for the conglomerates to establish their own financial institutions and thereby strengthen their base of autonomous finance. Furthermore, the opening up of Korea to foreign financial institutions gave Korean companies additional sources of finance. As businesses became less government dependent, they became more able to challenge the government when they felt it intervened too heavily.

With re-democratization (as of 1987), the balance of power between government and business changed yet further, and government was no longer in a position to dominate. Nationwide labor demonstration in the summer of 1987 and continuous strikes resulted in rapid wage increases.

Capital now had to work out a new strategy for dealing with stronger trade unions and to prevent or reduce industrial disputes without the help of government repression. The solution was closer labor coordination. Most large firms launched initiatives under slogans such as "management centered on human value" and "democratization of management." They increased personnel in departments to deal with trade unions, working conditions, and welfare issues, and the heads of such divisions were upgraded in management hierarchies.[50] A survey by the Council of Economic Organizations showed that, in late 1990, among 371 firms surveyed, 64 percent had specialized divisions dealing with labor relations and trade unions, most of them established after 1987.[51] For instance, in the Hyundai Motor Company, the largest motor company in Korea, the Division of Labor-Management Cooperation was separated from the Department of Personnel and became an independent department. Its main functions were to work toward the trade unions, to develop occupational welfare, and to improve industrial relations.[52]

Employers wanted unions under the control of moderate and pragmatic factions of workers. Management strategy was now to actively support union leadership as long as it stayed within the boundaries of pragmatic unionism. Thanks to the export boom and the expansion of domestic markets, as long as trade unions were cooperative, companies could well manage the extra costs of rising wages and additional occupational benefits.

This climate of cooperation between management and labor resulted in some improvements in working conditions. Enforced overtime work gradually disappeared. The separation of restaurants for production workers and clerical staff, which had been a symbol of discrimination against production workers, halted. Army-barrack-style labor controls (such as hair-length regulations) were relaxed. Most companies began to abolish the difference in the provision of bonuses and welfare benefits between production workers and managerial staff. New occupational welfare programs for production workers were introduced.

Changing sources of business finance loosened the relationship between business and the government further. The securities and stock markets exploded in the 1980s and became important sources of finance for large companies in particular. The number of companies listed in the stock exchange increased from about 350 at the beginning of the 1980s to 626 as of 1989. Listed capital increased from 2.4 trillion *won* in 1980 to 21.2 trillion *won* in 1989.[53] Growing corporate access to equity markets and non-bank intermediaries meant that businesses, particularly the *chaebŏl*, no longer had much need for direct government support.

With the Kim Young Sam government, the first civilian government after 1961, deregulation and *chaebŏl* reform became dominant themes of business policy, the former more successful than the latter. The combination of deregulation and a lenient stand on the *chaebŏl* resulted in liberalization without proper regulatory institutions and followed through to careless borrowing by many companies and the accumulation of massive foreign debt. Initial earnest attempts by the Kim government to institute more transparent business and financial practices gradually weakened or disappeared from the agenda, in the end possibly because the ruling party continued to depend heavily on *chaebŏl* financial support.

In January 1997, Hanbo, a major steel company, went bankrupt in a messy process that brought to light the depth of continuing government–business corruption, involving among others the son of the President. Throughout the year, as the Asian financial crisis took hold, businesses across the board destabilized, in part under the burden of debt. Foreign lenders lost confidence in Korean institutions and started to withdraw credit. *Chaebŏl* such as Sammi, Haitai, Jinro, Halla, and Daewoo and many smaller companies fell into bankruptcy.

In the aftermath of the shock of economic crisis and the election of Kim Dae Jung as president, it was finally possible to carry through (some) *chaebŏl* reform of a kind that had been off and on the political agenda since the Chun government. Through the Fair Trade Act, with four revisions, the government banned inter-subsidiary mutual payment guarantees and obliged the *chaebŏl* to clear their payment guarantees by March 2000. The monitoring and regulating role of the government was strengthened. A Fair Trade Commission was established and given access to information on financial transactions of the 30 largest *chaebŏl* from the National Tax Service. A more radical measure was the so-called "Big Deal" to get the top five *chaebŏl* to curb subsidiary activity and concentrate on their main industries. This took the direct intervention of President Kim personally, who summoned the leaders of these corporations and threatened them with legislation unless they volunteered to streamline their businesses.[54] These government measures were successful in curbing to some degree the diversification of the *chaebŏl*, and the average number of subsidiaries of the 10 largest *chaebŏl* decreased from 40 in 1997 to 32 in 2002.

LABOR

The labor movement was a constant force of pressure or irritation, depending on one's perspective, during the period of Korean development. There was a tradition of resistance dating back to Japanese colonization that persisted through authoritarian rule, with periodic bursts of activism and collective action, until government–labor relations gradually normalized under democratization. However, working-class organization never took off in Korea, neither in the form of leftist political parties of any force nor a powerful union movement, and labor was never to be a strong force in the reshaping of Korean economy and society. In part, labor organization was weak and fragmented, and the union movement suffered from endless internal strife and conflict and from authoritarianism and corruption in union leadership. Shifting authoritarian governments responded to union pressure and activism with manipulation, controls, and repression. Unions were confined, and confined themselves, to issues of workers' rights and wages, and were neither able nor inclined to engage with any force in broader issues of public policy. Social policy activism on the part of the authoritarian governments was initiated from above more than being shaped as a response to demands from organized labor. While governments engaged with capital in a developmental partnership, their dealing with labor was more one-sided: unions were controlled and held down.

A first significant step toward ordered labor relations was taken in 1953 with the adoption of four acts: the Trade Union Act, the Act on Mediation of Labor Disputes, the Labor Council Act, and the Labor Standards Act. The first three of these acts guaranteed workers' rights to association and collective action. However, clauses restricting the exercise of these rights were also included—for example, the right of the government to audit the financial operations of trade unions and to amend or invalidate decisions by trade union bodies. It promoted a corporate union system by confining collective bargaining to individual companies and banning third-party intervention—for example, picketing organized by non-firm unions. The ban on third-party intervention was to be a constant constraint on organized labor until democratization. The Act on Mediation of

Labor Disputes put mediation processes under government control. The Labor Council Act set up a Labor Council composed of representatives of government, employers, workers, and experts on labor affairs with a mandate to promote better working conditions.

The Trade Union Act would subsequently in periods be suspended—for example from 1961 to 1963 and from 1972 to 1981—and repeatedly modified according to shifting government needs, for example in 1963, 1964, 1973, 1987, and 1997. The Labor Standards Act regulated various minimum working conditions as obligations on employers; was for its time progressive on safety and health, working hours, and retirement pay; and included provisions to annul employment contracts that did not meet the standards of the Act. It was intensely contested by employers as economically unrealistic, and implementation was initially feeble and compliance in large measure ignored. However, this Act remained a powerful reference for labor in disputes over working conditions, was in periods used as an instrument of pressure by governments on employers to improve workers' conditions, and established principles of workers' welfare upon which later developments in occupational welfare could build. The Act was revised and extended in 1961, 1966, 1974, and 1975 and had a significant revision in 1997.

Two national level labor organizations were established shortly after independence: the General Council of Korean Trade Unions, leaning toward the left, and the Labor Federation for Independence, leaning toward the right. Both organizations were leadership controlled, and neither had much membership strength.[55] A purge of left-wing unions after 1947 left the Labor Federation in command, and with the Trade Union Act of 1953 it became the legitimized national union, eventually under the name of the Federation of Korean Trade Unions (FKTU). Persistent internal strife and political divisions, however, significantly undermined its capacity to function as an organization with national clout.

The short period from the collapse of the Rhee government to the 1961 coup was one of intense labor activism. New unions were formed, unionization increased, and strikes and demonstrations proliferated. Workers turned against union leaders who had been collaborating with the Rhee government, many of whom were forced to resign. New unions took more effective action on economic demands, often with reference to the Labor Standards Act. For example, the National Teachers' Union, the most significant of the new unions, made demands on family and health allowances, and the Railway Workers' Union obtained increases in both wages and allowances for dangerous duty.[56]

Labor activism came to an end with the military coup in 1961. As with other political organizations, trade unions were disbanded and many union leaders arrested. The junta quickly revised the Trade Union Act in 1961 and 1963 and restructured the union system.[57] Initially, 12 new industrial sector unions were formed and a new Federation of Korean Trade Unions established as the national organization. Existing firm-level trade unions were reorganized as branches of the new industrial sector unions. One of the most damaging clauses for unionism was the empowerment of the government to overrule the lawfulness of industrial action. A cooling-off period of 20 days in industrial disputes was imposed, during which the government would be able to intervene and impose a settlement. Trade unions were put under almost complete government control. By 1971, only 13 percent of employees were union members.[58]

Until democratization, unionism had its strength, such as it was, at the firm level. Here, unions were able to engage in negotiations, if within restricted scope and under constantly shifting circumstances, and to organize splinter groups. Bursts of labor militancy mostly originated at this level. Industry-level unions, such as textile, chemical, metal, and automobile workers' unions, were generally prevented by authoritarian restrictions from mobilizing for collective action. Negotiations, when available, were limited to the individual firm, could not be backed up by external support or threat of action, and were mostly settled by formal or informal government intervention.

The Federation of Korean Trade Unions focused during this period on legal questions of workers' and union rights more than on wages and welfare issues. Even so, it did have some achievements on social issues. Among these, a notable success was its resistance against provisions in the Bill for the Promotion of the Capital Market, which would have enabled state-owned enterprises to pay retirement pay and bonuses in the form of stocks and bonds in an immature and highly fluctuating stock market. Another achievement was to get the issue of a minimum wage established on the agenda.[59] It was proposed in 1969 and, although not accepted then, became a reference for subsequent collective bargaining and action.

While controlling union activity, the junta moved to improving working conditions by revising the Labor Standards Act in December 1961. Retirement pay (of no less than 30 days of the average wage per year for the number of consecutive years employed by the company) was made compulsory for firms with more than 30 employees, as was maternity leave. For employees under 18, employers were required either to provide schooling or pay school fees. An Office of Labor Affairs was established as an independent ministry to strengthen the government's ability to mediate in labor disputes and to prevent the eruption of conflict. However, although the law was improved, practical follow-ups were patchy. Most employers did not comply, and implementation was under less than intense scrutiny by the government.

From 1969 onward, in response to increasing labor unrest, the government employed harsher measures against activism. A Special Law on Labor in Foreign Invested Firms banned most union activities in these firms. Then followed in 1971 the Special Decree for National Security, which banned union activity in any firm deemed by the government to be strategically important, and in 1972 the State of Emergency by which all collective labor rights were suspended, including obviously the right to strike but also to engage in any other industrial action that was seen to be disruptive to social order. The *Yushin* constitution severely restricted any right of association.

The 1973 revision of the Trade Union Act again stipulated a corporate structure of firm-based unions. Then, as a measure to further undermine union power or even any role for unions, it imposed an obligation on (larger) firms to establish Labor Management Councils to deal with issues of production, education, job training, working conditions, workers' grievances, and related matters. These Councils would be prioritized meeting arenas of workers and managers and effectively deny unions any space of operation at the firm level. They came to function mainly as channels for employers to impose their will on workers. By 1979, more than 13,000 firms had such councils, more than three times the number that had trade unions.[60]

The 1974 and 1975 revisions of the Labor Standards Act contributed to further reducing the role of unions but also enforced on employers a duty to improve working conditions. This was partly in response to increasing discontent, in particular in smaller companies at the end of the export production chain. The application of the Act was extended, required standards improved, and penalties for noncompliance made heavier. The government also broadened the coverage of the Industrial Accident Insurance so that by 1979 3.6 million workers were covered, up from initially about 80,000 workers in 1964. Although compliance continued to lag far behind the letter of the law, working conditions did in at least some respects improve.

In 1973, the government launched the Factory *Saemaul* Movement as a proactive intervention in industrial relations with the aim of promoting industrial morale. This grew out of the successful prior rural initiative in the *Saemaul* Movement. Institutions of deliberation were set up, both nationally and locally and within and outside of factories, to involve rafts of people from top-level government officials down to workers and family members, and for the purpose of instilling work ethics and cooperative attitudes. Some of these institutions, particularly those on the national level, were tripartite organizations of government, employers, and workers that dealt with a wide range of matters such as wages, working conditions, safety and health, and the special needs of female and young workers.

Contrary to industrial bargaining, these deliberations became regularized with the strong support of employers. Occupational welfare issues were now actively discussed and could often be decided through this channel. Unions were again sidelined and steered increasingly to making demands for better protection from the "benevolent state," whose control over labor leadership in return became further consolidated.

Two divergent trends within the labor movement emerged from this institutional framework: a sanctioned union leadership preoccupied with economic and business unionism, and more-or-less underground activists who questioned the legitimacy of the leadership and demanded union autonomy from both government and employers, referred to as "the democratic union movement."

The interim between President Park's assassination in October 1979 and martial law in May 1980 brought this ideological and political division to the surface. Activists turned against corrupt and time-serving leaders who dominated organized labor, sometimes by voting them out and sometimes with physical violence. New unions were formed, workers and students took to the streets, and demonstrations and riots proliferated. But not for long. With martial law as of May 1980, the democratic union movement was crushed and labor activists were subjected to arrest or surveillance. Industrial relations were forced back into Labor Management Councils that were now more explicitly than previously mandated to deal with the whole agenda of productivity enhancement, occupational welfare, vocational training, disputes, grievances, safety and health, working conditions, labor-management cooperation, and so on.

In June 1987, when Roh Tae Woo as the establishment presidential candidate opened up for comprehensive democratization measures, labor activism immediately surfaced again and strikes broke out in both large and small companies nationwide. Worker demands included not only better wages and conditions but also freedom of association and of industrial action. In November, the National Assembly relaxed labor law restrictions on union formation and activity and reduced government intervention in industrial relations. The unions regained priority status over Labor Management Councils as the main bargaining counterpart. Although this was a great step forward for labor and the unions, there were still limitations. One was that the law preserved the banning of third-party intervention in disputes, which effectively prevented national or industrial-level unions from engaging with labor relations at the firm level. Another clause prohibited the formation of new unions in firms with existing unions, something that protected the position of the unions that were established and had worked under the authoritarian regime.[61] Thus the privileged status of the old unions, particularly national and industrial-level unions, was perpetuated. The stage was set for a showdown between the established unions and the democratic trade union movement, a showdown the government was unwittingly to orchestrate in late 1996 and early 1997.

Wage negotiations under the new framework of industrial relations in the spring of 1988 were marred by strikes, violence, dismissals, and police interference. Old corporate institutions were re-mobilized and new ones set up to deflect labor unrest, such as the Central Labor Management Council, the Minimum Wage Consultation Committee, and the National Committee for Economic and Social Affairs. These brought together government officials, employers, and trade union leaders, mostly under the auspices of the Federation of Korean Trade Unions. As only consultative bodies, however, they could not hammer out binding agreements. The government was still hesitant to allow national-level trade unions any real participation in policy making. Privileged national-level unions were lacking in capacity to represent the working class. The movement of emerging democratic unions clustered in an independent umbrella organization, the National Council for the Revision of Labor Laws.

From 1989, economic growth slowed, exports became sluggish, and widespread strikes damaged production. Employers demanded a harder hand from the government in response to strikes. The FKTU tried to strengthen its legitimacy by getting actively behind demonstrations and demands for revisions of labor laws, better social protection, fairer taxation, and increased wages.

The government, strengthened by the successful Seoul Olympics and boosted in legitimacy by probes to investigate Fifth Republic corruption, turned to tougher measures on strikes in the name of law and order. This, however, further politicized the democratic movement, which turned its struggle into a more explicitly anti-government one. The FKTU was forced on the defensive and had to compete with a highly politicized counterpart on the agenda it was able to define.[62]

Under President Kim Young Sam, the government again relaxed its interference in industrial relations and promoted dialogue between national organizations of labor and employers. The only recognized national level trade union, the FKTU, now pushed for a tripartite dialogue also involving the government. The half-hearted attitude of the government and workers' distrust of the FKTU leadership, however, caused the attempt at broader social dialogue and tripartism to peter out. More unions withdrew from FKTU membership and aligned with the democratic movement. In 1995, a new national-level organization was set up, the Korean Confederation of Trade Unions. Although initially smaller than FKTU—about 400,000 members, a fourth of the organized workforce—it had power in force of legitimacy and a more activist base.

It was now, under the Kim government, that the powerfully symbolic issue of labor market "flexibility" was pushed to the top of the industrial relations agenda. Business and government saw flexibility on, for example, job security and working hours as necessary in order to retain competitiveness in the face of economic globalization. The government set up a new consultative body, the Presidential Commission for Industrial Relations Reform, with representatives of both employers and unions, now also the Korean Confederation of Trade Unions (although still technically not a legal organization). The Commission failed to reach consensus. The government went on to legislate regardless, but in a provocative and manipulative manner (see Chapter 5). Large-scale strikes followed in early 1997 in a campaign in which the FKTU was forced to join the KCTU in militant activism. The government caved in and suspended the legislation it had pushed through, and the issue of flexibility was left unresolved.

Financial crisis hit Korea in late 1997 and changed the structure of industrial relations significantly. Flexibility was enforced as part of the IMF bailout package and was implemented under President Kim Dae Jung. He established the Tripartite Commission, with the participation of both national unions. After painstaking negotiations under serious time constraint, the parties in early 1998 agreed to a face-saving compromise with essentially the same flexibility measures that had been dismissed a year earlier. This signaled the end of lifelong employment in big enterprises. In return, labor obtained improved unemployment insurance and social assistance, and the Korean Confederation of Trade Unions (KCTU) gained full legal recognition.[63]

Korea overcame the financial crisis earlier than expected, but with increased insecurity of employment as a lasting effect. With democratic consolidation, government–union relations normalized. Direct government interference in union activity and industrial relations was scaled back, and trade unions both nationally and at the firm level could work normally within normal industrial relations.

OCCUPATIONAL WELFARE

The Korean brand of occupational welfare was a product of political authoritarianism. It was a system of control over employers to make them deliver for workers on behalf of the government, and over workers to keep the lid on labor discontentment and potential unrest. It was ideologically based, grounded in moralistic principles of work ethics and self-reliance. The escape from poverty was to come through discipline and industry. Benefits, not only wages but also security, should be obtained through work and be framed to encourage work and reward effort. It was a device for combining social responsiveness with single-minded promotion of economic growth. It was designed to help prevent a pressure-cooker economy from going off the rails. It was imposed from above on more or less willing labor market "partners."

The system stood on two pillars. First, social insurance. The government legislated for insurance programs that were imposed on employers and workers and which they themselves had to pay for and mostly manage. Second, corporatist paternalism. In addition to social insurance, the government partly imposed and partly cajoled a familial enterprise spirit in which workers asked for rather than demanded benefits—hence the repression of unionization and collective action—and employers were made to provide in-kind benefits to workers on top of, or sometimes instead of, wages. Enforced familialism is an odd idea but a powerful one under Korean authoritarianism.

The Korean welfare state was for a long time in the main confined to occupational welfare (and to voluntary agency welfare, as we explore in the next chapter).

Not until democratic consolidation did the state seriously start to make itself a provider of welfare.

The system of social insurance we have covered in the previous chapter: in order, industrial accident and tentative health insurance, followed by national pensions and unemployment compensation.

All through the authoritarian period, unions were held down as an independent source of political power. Obedient labor organizations were privileged but given a very restricted space of operation. From the early 1950s, relatively progressive laws were in place on working conditions, in particular the Labor Standards Act. Authoritarian governments would in periods use this legislation as the reverse side of the repression of workers' rights to force employers to improve working conditions more than they were inclined to. This did not necessarily translate into what might be considered, even for the time, conspicuously good working conditions, but it did contribute to visible improvements for workers and to making conditions better than they could have been.

Corporate paternalism was fortified in the New Factory Community Movement, which was remarkably successful as a campaign of mass mobilization and generated various improvement projects in and around workplaces across the country. One outgrowth, for example, was a Workers' Savings Scheme in 1976, based on a minimal subvention of interest, with more than 800,000 participants within nine months. Another was the formation of cooperative societies to provide employees with goods at subsidized prices. These were in operation in more than 1,000 companies by 1979.[64]

Linked with efforts to enhance productivity, companies were encouraged to establish firm-based educational facilities and schools to establish evening class programs for workers. Other manifestations of paternalism were workplace meals, clothing, and sports, recreational and bath facilities, all of which were provided by a majority of firms.

Non-statutory mostly in-kind occupational benefits were in the late 1970s estimated to account for between 5 and 7 percent of total labor costs, as compared, for example, to less than 2 percent for employer contributions to Industrial Accident and National Health Insurance.[65]

The Chun government's trumpeting of "the welfare state" did in fact follow through to a modest increase in government social spending, but it was still primarily the occupational welfare sector that was to expand. In most companies, Labor Management Councils became the main institutions for the promotion of occupational welfare. In 1981 the government issued a "guideline" on company welfare facilities that stipulated details of expected provisions in at least larger companies. The costs of occupational welfare increased significantly as a share of total labor cost. For example, the costs of non-statutory occupational welfare in mining and manufacturing industries increased from 5 percent of total labor cost in 1979 to 6.5 percent on average in the years from 1982 to 1987.[66]

Employers did not always bend to the government's will. In a notable case in 1982, the Korea Employers Federation successfully resisted an attempt by the government to impose by legislation compulsory Company Welfare Funds to be used for the benefit of workers but funded by employers. This time the government backed down and instead resorted again to a "guideline" on the establishment of welfare funds at the discretion of management and workers. On a promise of tax concessions, companies were encouraged to set aside up to 5 percent of profits in funds to be run by Labor Management Councils and used for loans or subventions to employees for purposes such as housing or children's education. This guideline was, however, not successful in mobilizing compliance by employers, and Company Welfare Funds were set up in only a small minority of firms.

By the time of democratization, occupational welfare was firmly entrenched as the core of the welfare state and has so remained. From 1986 to 1992, the share in total labor costs of statuary social insurance contributions and voluntary occupational benefits increased from 2.2 to 4.4 percent and 6.7 to 9.0 percent, respectively (in companies with 30 or more employees).[67]

In the early 1990s, the Korean economy showed signs of overheating. The government responded with attempted wage controls, but with little success. Unions were now stronger, and large companies in particular preferred to accept their wage demands over strikes and the interruption of production. The wage gap between workers in large and small companies widened. This continued under Kim Young Sam, again in the face of unsuccessful measures to restrain wage increases. Economic recovery from 1993 gave further impetus to union wage demands. During Kim's tenure, wages increased by more than 10 percent per year on average. Occupational welfare costs continued to increase, but now less than wages.

The financial crisis brought a (temporary) end to the wage boom, but while average wages were down drastically in 1998 (by 8.3 percent), total wage costs increased (by 12.2 percent) due to a rise in the cost of retirement pay and also of statutory social insurance contributions.

In the now more flexible labor market, non-regular workers accounted for more than 20 percent of all employees at the most conservative estimate. Job security was undermined and layoffs became more common. Inequalities continued to increase, including in occupational welfare, since non-regular workers have much less access to such benefits and supports than do regular workers.[68]

Democratization did not result in any discontinuation of occupational welfare. Social insurance programs continued and matured, as did the system of occupational benefits beyond statutory insurance. What did change in workplaces was that the paternalistic structure of occupational welfare was rolled back. Unionization was normalized and occupational benefits subjected to more balanced negotiation and agreements, and in some cases turned into statutory rights. What changed in the welfare state was less in occupational welfare than in additions to occupational welfare as the state took on new responsibilities of provision.

CORPORATIST MIXED GOVERNANCE

By the end of the century, government–capital–labor relations had settled down to normalcy. The legacies of the developmental state disappeared, and the government aimed to properly supervise a proper market economy. But the road thereto had been tumultuous and complicated. It started with the replacement of the old landowning class by a new class of independent farmers that prospered by "supplying" labor to industrial development. It progressed by way of crude cronyism into a particular brand of *chaebŏl* monopoly capitalism, under the stewardship of a tiny elite with immense economic power, a power the authoritarian rulers had the wisdom to accommodate themselves to and co-opt. It is here we see the reliance of the developmental state on mixed governance. That state elite chose, in spite of itself, to cooperate with a business elite it despised, although it was more or less of its own creation. These two antagonistic powers worked together by mutually selling out to each other.

During the authoritarian period, the strong state made itself extraordinarily dominant as the driver of economic and industrial development, but also found itself dependent on the economic actors it subdued. Gradually, with economic growth and increasing business sophistication, the grip of the authoritarian state loosened. Government–capital relations had, however, never taken the form of one-sided command, even under the hardest authoritarianism, but were always, albeit in shifting ways, tugs of war regulated by give and take, tacit and explicit negotiations, compromises and pervasive two-way corruption. Rapid industrialization created a huge working class that, however, left little imprint on Korean development except by that of its toil and exploitation. It was unable to organize with notable force, be it in unionization or political representation, and rarely made itself more than an irritant, although at times thoroughly so. Labor organization has remained weak in Korea, as if industrialization progressed too rapidly for labor to keep apace. The remarkable thing is that out of this unlikely nexus of class conflict, criss-crossing distrust, and repression came not economic chaos and implosion but workable corporatism and, gradually, economic–political normalization.

4

THE STATE MEETS VOLUNTARISM

The discovery that Korea has been ruled not only through a coalition of government and business but also in a second coalition of government and civil society is both surprising and not surprising. It is not surprising in the sense that
Korea has been governed effectively and that effective governance never flows
directly from the state, however strong that state may be. Where there is successful governance there are always other contributing actors. The Korean story
could not have unfolded as it did if the state had been only a command state; it
had to be also a collaborative state. As so often, when one is minded to look, one
finds. Once we set ourselves to search for the Korean civil society and its contribution to the development of the nation, we found a great deal of activity and
contribution to pull into the broader analysis.

There is nevertheless also surprise in this discovery. Korea emerged from colonization, war, and civil war a destroyed nation. One might think it therefore a
nation without much civil structure to mobilize, and for that reason exceptionally dependent on the state, and that it became so typically a state-led society
because there were no other actors to offer leadership. But that is not the case.
Voluntarism emerged immediately as the nation itself started to emerge.

The conventional narrative of Korean political history awards very little role
to anyone but the state and business. However, there was from the start much
more to the political fabric of Korea; there has also been an equally important
vibrant network of voluntary agencies. The strong state dominated these agencies, but they also, as in the case of business, let themselves be dominated at a
price. As did business, voluntary agencies extracted concessions from the state

that depended on them as an instrument of its rule. The state needed to get social services delivered but did not have the means to do so itself. Voluntary agencies took on this job. They did that under state direction but were also able to create a domain of their own and to grow and prosper.

THE VOLUNTARY SECTOR

It has been suggested that voluntary organizations managed to become notable social actors in Korea as a result of the democratic transition from the late 1980s and that the authoritarian state had allowed little or no space for an active voluntary sector.[69] But that is not correct. The voluntary sector was established in Korea before the authoritarian period, was not put out of play by the coming of authoritarian rule, and continued into the re-emergence of democracy.

The sector has always been a mixed bag in Korea. War and underdevelopment held back the emergence of indigenous voluntary agencies. Voluntarism was initially associated with, on the one hand, an informal arrangement of social networks based upon family, kinship, community self-help, and religiously motivated voluntary work, and on the other hand foreign agencies in more formalized agency work. It came to be guided and controlled by state intervention and deliberately mobilized to cover for the state in service delivery. In the run-up to re-democratization in the 1980s, service provision to some degree became overshadowed by advocacy-oriented groups that mushroomed in the wake of the 1987 June Uprising, emphasizing proactive advocacy functions, including the broadening of public debate and political participation in the formation of public policy. Social policy issues were deliberately politicized for the purpose of mobilizing forces from below in the democratic transition.

Our first task here is to give a detailed description of this unknown component of Korean political life and governance. The voluntary sector itself is one of the least understood and least conceptualized parts of social policy studies. Lack of clear categorization and definition extends to even the variation of the generic terms used to identify the sector in various countries.[70] The need to avoid becoming entangled with unproductive debates over semantics calls for a mixed approach to defining the voluntary sector in the Korean context. While using the *broad* conceptualization developed by the Johns Hopkins Comparative Nonprofit Sector Project as the default definition of the voluntary sector by international criteria, we also focus on some distinctive characters of the Korean voluntary agencies as *specific* explanatory factors. The former covers societal organizations that are formal, nonprofit, distributing, constitutionally independent of the state, self-governing, and benefiting from voluntarism.[71] As for particularities in the Korean context, at least three are essential. First, Korea's voluntary sector has been intimately associated with informal sectors and is as such not a single institutional sector. Second, the activities of voluntary organizations—at least prior to democratization—were often involuntarily guided and controlled by strong intervention from the state. Third, voluntary service provision was in periods overshadowed and even marginalized by advocacy-oriented groups that became dominant in Korean civil society in the re-democratization period.

By the year 2000, *The Korean NGO Yearbook* sets the number of civil society organizations to 4,023, rising to about 20,000 if their local branches are counted. Among them, there were 965 voluntary associations specified to social services and community development, which is equivalent to 24 percent of the total of civic groups. Recent research credits the voluntary sector in Korea as a considerable economic force, albeit with comparatively modest institutional capacity by the standards of the most developed countries.[72] Measured by expenditure, the economic size of the sector was the equivalent nearly to 5 percent of gross domestic product, well in excess of the government's social expenditure in 1997.[73] In employment, the sector generated about 700,000 full-time equivalent jobs, more than 3 percent of the economically active population and the equivalent of half of public employment. About 82 percent of the voluntary sector workforce in 1997 was engaged in social and educational service delivery.

Foreign Relief Agencies

The Korean War shattered tightly knit village communities. The alleviation of dire poverty, such as it was, was left to an influx of foreign, mainly American, relief agencies. By 1961, the combined annual budget of foreign agencies was more than twice that of the Ministry of Health and Social Affairs. The number of foreign voluntary agencies reached a peak of about 120 in 1965. In 1952, they formed the Korean Association of Voluntary Agencies to enhance and coordinate relief efforts.[74] Voluntarism started as a foreign import. It was gradually taken over by Korean agencies, but the foreign influence was to last. With the retreat of foreign agencies, the system of the Korean Association of Voluntary Agencies broke down—its secretariat ceased to operate in 1976—but the example left behind a precedent of centrally coordinated voluntarism that was to be revived later with re-democratization.

The main focus of foreign aid was in social welfare. By 1959, nine out of ten welfare facilities in the country were operated by voluntary organizations, most of which received financial and material support from abroad.[75] Facilities for the protection of children became the top priority, including infant homes, orphanages, day nurseries, child guidance clinics, and reformatory schools. This bequeathed two behavioral patterns on the next generation of the voluntary sector. Firstly, the traditional culture of welfare services was transformed from a Confucian elderly-oriented system to children-centered services. Secondly, the emphasis on facility-based solutions to social protection problems drew agencies toward reactive social work and the segregation of social underdogs from the mainstream of society, and away from long-term preventive programs and efforts designed at the integration and rehabilitation of disadvantaged people into work and social participation more broadly.

The foreign influence was very much an American influence. The Korean voluntary sector was to share the essence of American voluntarism, with the emphasis on philanthropic, apolitical, and charity-oriented service and individual aid rather than the building of comprehensive systems of social support and security.[76] The philanthropic design was influenced by a Christianity-based religious grounding of foreign voluntarism. Most of the agencies worked within Protestant or Catholic missionary projects and by and large saw their mission as one of secular charity for posthumous salvation. Originally in the hands of non-professional social workers, and with a distrust of professional social work, foreign voluntarism gradually brought more professionals to Korea, predominantly trained in American universities. Their lasting influence was a pro-American intellectual elite in the emerging Korean voluntary sector and the reproduction there of American standards of social welfare services as a model for Korean voluntarism.

Authoritarian Rule

The advent of military authoritarianism in 1961 brought in a tighter regulation of voluntary groups. The military regime monopolized all channels of policy coordination by installing in 1962 the National Relief Coordination Committee and similar provincial committees throughout the country.[77] The consequence of state regulation was the eventual retreat of foreign agencies from the late 1960s.

The voluntary sector, however, survived and persisted but also degenerated into a quasi-extended arm of the state.[78] The retreat of foreign voluntarism reduced the flow of money from abroad and left the sector more dependent on government finance and bound to comply with government conditions. When the Park government in the 1970s rolled out the *Saemaul* Movement, it was able to saddle voluntary groups and local communities with extensive social responsibilities. This contributed to further tying voluntary groups down to service provision, to limiting their involvement to a narrow niche of social work, and to keeping them away from social welfare deliberations more broadly, not to mention political advocacy.

The voluntary sector perforce became cautiously sensitive to the rules and expectations that were defined by the state. In a typical case of what has been called "coercive isomorphism," this tendency became internalized in voluntary culture as an adaptation to formal and informal pressures from above and normative expectations from the broader civil society.[79] The state exerted direct influence on voluntarism by setting up public interest corporations as legally distinct from the apparatus proper of government. A classical example was the National Council of *Saemaul* Movements, which acted as an umbrella representative and coordinator of more than 35,000 community-based local groups and members. It also exerted control and influence indirectly by stimulating the upgrowth of welfare foundations in the corporate sector as a part of its strategic adaptation to authoritarian rule. The *Yushin* authorities stressed the social responsibility of private companies by pressuring them to return some of their profit to society in general and to employees in particular. Private firms would resist government pressure to set up company welfare funds but complied by establishing philanthropic foundations for societal purposes as defensive vehicles vis-à-vis the state. The number of such foundations throughout the corporate sector increased rapidly during the 1970s, when most of the large corporations set up their own social and cultural foundations, about half of whose spending went into the provision of social services.[80]

Voluntary welfare services under the Park regime were in large measure a continuation of foreign voluntary activities, but with some notable changes. Child welfare remained the primary concern, and working through welfare facilities remained the predominant methodology, but with modifications. There was a move to deinstitutionalize welfare services for children. The 1961 Child Welfare Act prioritized the care of children in their families or communities.[81] Welfare institutes for children were slowly discontinued—reduced in number, for example, from 523 in 1970 to 279 in 1985—not only due to the decrease in child abandonment, but also in favor of personalized services for children, such as day care services and day nurseries. A part of the rationale for this move toward more modern child care was a desire to mobilize more women into industrial labor with the help of better day care services for children. Furthermore, the voluntary sector strove to diversify its services to other areas than child services. Among new agencies established in this period, more were directed to elderly or disabled services.

The second military regime headed by Chun Doo Hwan sought legitimacy in a pledge to "the building of a welfare state." The promise of proactive public welfare was followed by a series of laws to expand service coverage to a wider range of socially excluded groups, including the disabled, the elderly, single mothers, vagrants, and so on, but not by any noticeable increase in public social spending. The corresponding development in the voluntary sector came as a combination of "horizontal" and "vertical" expansion.[82] More voluntary groups came into social work, contributing to the diversification of service content and a widening range of service recipients, with in particular more activity in welfare services for the disabled. At the same time, various central or national coordinating agencies were created or took on a new assertiveness. The Korean National Council on Social Welfare had been established already in 1952 and was now able to re-mobilize its vertical channels. By 1985 it had 16 regional offices and 90 local branches in operation. The Korean Association of Social Workers, established in 1967, revamped 16 regional bureaus into liaison offices in order to facilitate more effective communication and coordination between local and central agencies. These national umbrella organizations played a significant role not only in coordinating voluntary involvement throughout the country but also, for example, in organizing training programs for social workers, generating more vertical contact and exchange, and marshalling protection of their rights and interests against external intervention.

The expansion of voluntary networks in the mid-1980s conveyed dual images of the voluntary sector to the state: a latent warehouse of social challenge against the authoritarian government on the one hand, and on the other hand a potential bank of human resources for service delivery in cooperation with the statutory sector. The resultant reaction from the Chun regime was the incorporation of key voluntary national networks into the statutory delivery system of social services that the Ministry of Health and Social Affairs controlled. Furthermore, the financial shakiness and amateurish staff of the voluntary sector undermined confidence in its operational capacity, independently from state intervention. Consequently, some vertical networks of voluntary groups in this period deepened their dependency on state inducements, eventually acting as an extended ladder of the integrated delivery channels combining the central government and local service groups. This nascent form of state–voluntary partnerships turned some voluntary umbrellas into conservative supporters of state policies in ways that were to endure after the coming of democratization in the late 1980s.

Democratic Transition

With the democratic breakthrough in 1987, the landscape of civil society and voluntarism changed dramatically. Coalitions of activism by trade unions, religious groups, and university students had brought the authoritarian regime down. The voluntary sector no longer needed to see itself as a state instrument but could take on a proactive role in public discussion on social policy and political advocacy.

What followed was an explicit politicization of welfare agendas. Civil organizations on social justice, human rights, environmental degradation, and women's rights proliferated, including a raft of varied and more or less organized social welfare movements working for the remedy of inequalities in distribution and deficiencies in public welfare schemes.[83] The range, magnitude, and force of such movements are illustrated in Table 3. A voluntary sector that had previously looked subdued took to advocacy with astonishing speed, energy, and delight. It also proved apt in advocacy organization. National voluntary coalition networks were formed. Characteristically, the People's Solidarity for Participatory Democracy, founded in 1994, played a pioneering role in bringing problems of distribution and inequality to the front of its political advocacy, set in motion the Committee on Social Welfare under the slogan of "welfare is not a social benefit, but a social right," and organized for increased public social spending.

Key voluntary organizations began to participate directly in social policy decision making. The state responded to the politicization of welfare issues by incorporating leading voluntary federations into policy procedures on two

Table 3: Historical Development of Social Welfare Movements

Year	Contents
1988	Social welfare movements for the protection of the rights to life
1989	Petition movements for Employment Promotion Act for the Disabled, Welfare Act for the Mentally and Physically Disabled, and the Basic Law for the Youth Political struggle for the poor in the slum districts
1990	Social welfare movements for the democratic operation of welfare facilities Social welfare movements for signing the UN Convention on the Rights of the Child
1991	Political struggles for securing welfare facilities Petition movements for the Childcare Act (particularly, social care for infants)
1992	Social welfare movements for the protection of the educational rights of the disabled
1994	First petition to the National Assembly for the adoption of the Community Chest Law People's Solidarity for Participatory Democracy's movements for securing the government budget for social welfare programs People's Solidarity for Participatory Democracy's lawsuits against the mismanagement of the National Pension Program, the Livelihood Protection Programs, etc.
1995	The public hearing organized by 59 civic groups for the petitions concerning the legislations associated with the Volunteer Act, Community Chest Law, the Voluntary Movement Aid Act, and the Ban on Charitable Fundraisings Petition movements for the Basic Law for Women's Development, and the revision of the Welfare Act for the Elderly and the Livelihood Protection Law The second petition to the National Assembly for the adoption of the Community Chest Law
1996	The third petition to the National Assembly for the adoption of the Community Chest Law Social welfare movements for a national network promoting the rights of the disabled Social welfare movements for securing the professional status of social workers
1997	Petition movements for the revision of the 1991 Childcare Act and Social Welfare Service Act Petition movements for Regulations Concerning the Promotion and Protection of Welfare Facilities for the Disabled, the Elderly, and Expectant and Nursing Mothers Social welfare movements for the promotion of convenient facilities for the disabled
1998	Petition movements for the National Basic Livelihood Security Act: the launch of the National Convention of the Petition for Enacting the National Basic Livelihood Security Act Social welfare movements for supporting the unemployed and the homeless: launch of the Committee on the Citizen's Movement for Overcoming Unemployment Social welfare movements for the protection of part-time job mothers & maternity welfare
1999	Integrated social welfare movements for the National Basic Livelihood Security Act: the launch of the Solidarity for Enactment of the National Basic Livelihood Security Act
2000	Social welfare movements for self-support programs aimed at women and the poor People's Solidarity for Participatory Democracy's movements for the reform of institutional regulations about the public welfare schemes

(continued)

Table 3: Historical Development of Social Welfare Movements (*cont.*)

Year	Contents
2001	Social welfare movements for self-support programs aimed at the disabled Petition movements for the Handicapped Discrimination Prevention Act
2002	Open hearing of the presidential candidates organized by the Korean Association of Social Workers and the Disabled Coalition for the Presidential Election
2004	Anti-national pension movements

Sources: Kim (2007: 221, 295); Yi (2005: 43–61). Modification added.

different levels. The first track was involvement in agenda-setting functions. In three consecutive years from 1994 to 1996, 59 voluntary associations came together to push through public hearings and otherwise for a Community Chest Law to safeguard the distribution of voluntary donations to needy persons and families. The law was passed in the National Assembly in March 1997, resulting in the establishment of the Community Chest of Korea as a national umbrella organization with 16 local branches.

The second track was the setting up of joint committees of government agencies and voluntary associations. The Roh Tae Woo administration set up the Welfare Policy Committee for the Disabled and the Welfare Policy Committee for the Elderly, both under the chairmanship of the prime minister and including experts and representatives of voluntary organizations.[84] The role of voluntary associations in these governmental committees was developed further during the Kim Young Sam administration into a more hands-on participation in deliberation over and review of the general direction of the state welfare. In 1995, the Ministry of Health and Welfare established the Consultation Committee on Social Security of government officials and civic groups for regular reviews of welfare reform. The Planning Committee on Citizens' Welfare was set up the same year to pull voluntary groups into considerations over state and civil society collaboration in service delivery.[85] All in all, the participatory engagement of the voluntary sector in the public discourse of social policy facilitated voluntary contributions to constructing new institutional arrangements of welfare programs and state–civil society partnerships for them.

The scramble for political advocacy came, however, at the price of discord and disunity within the voluntary sector between the more conventional service-oriented and more progressive advocacy-oriented groups. Such an internal disjointedness and the lack of common ground between old and new voluntary groups undermined the capacity of the voluntary sector to call for the restructuring of public welfare services. Rather, disunity allowed the government to incorporate conventional welfare groups into strategic partnerships and to use differentiated institutional arrangements for handling the two branches of voluntarism.

Economic Crisis

The social distress resulting from the Asian financial crisis in 1997 and its entail-ing welfare vacuums called into question the existing public welfare system. By 1998, the unemployment rate had reached 6.8 percent. Income inequality increased sharply—the Gini coefficient for the distribution of income rose from 0.28 in 1995 to 0.32 in 1999—and the incidence of poverty reached almost 20 percent.[86] The Kim Dae Jung government's paradigm of "productive welfare" stressed the participatory contributions of civic actors in fostering community renewal in conjunction with a more activist program of state welfare. The volun-tary sector maintained its now-established dual role of advocacy and service provision, but pressing social fallouts and exclusions resulting from the crisis again put heavy demands on voluntary agencies for elementary relief work.

In the terrain of advocacy, voluntary sector actors pushed for a more compre-hensive understanding of rights, social inclusion, citizenship, and social policy. Voluntary groups were intimately involved in political processes leading up to the National Basic Livelihood Security Act. A first attempt, through the National Convention of the Petition for Enacting the National Basic Livelihood Security Act in 1998, ended in failure, but a second coalition, the Solidarity for Enacting the National Basic Livelihood Security Act, formed by 64 major voluntary associations in March 1999, was instrumental in marshaling the government's acceptance of universal minimum livelihood protection.

As a service provider, the voluntary sector played a critical role in providing crisis-driven welfare relief and community activism. Local welfare groups proliferated, aiming to promote self-support programs—primarily vocational rehabilitation services and job training plans for the unemployed and the new poor. A second target was an increase in homelessness in urban areas. The National Council of Religious and Civic Organizations for the Homeless and Unemployed was set up in May 1998 to coordinate welfare services such as emergency shelters, free meals, medical support, and self-help programs. The Food Bank, devised by the Ministry of Health and Welfare to distribute free food services to those most seriously marginalized and operated in collaboration with the voluntary sector, was another institutional channel for voluntary groups. A final pattern of voluntary participation in post-crisis service provisions was in the so-called self-support aid program, which was introduced as a supportive device for the National Basic Livelihood Security Act. The program was designed as a hybrid scheme to combine the welfare-to-work and income protection inten-tions of the National Basic Livelihood Security Act.[87] Self-support aid centers were set up by local welfare groups with financial and administrative support from the state. The number of such centers increased from about 20 in 1999 to 242 in 2005. All in all, social provision via the voluntary sector in post-crisis Korean society could be seen as micro-productive contributions to supplement macro-level state-run welfare schemes.[88]

The social fallouts of the financial crisis acted as a catalyst for the voluntary sector to strengthen its base of operation by both better intra-sector cooperation between agencies and new patterns of inter-sector cooperation between state and voluntary agencies. The Committee on the Citizen's Movement for Overcoming Unemployment was launched in June 1998 by a wide range of religious groups, civic associations, trade unions, professional scholars, and local welfare organizations, spearheaded by three religious leaders—Cardinal Kim Su-Hwan of the Korean Catholic Church, Reverend Kang Wŏn-Yong, and Executive Chief Song Wŏl-Ju of the Korean Buddhist Chogye Order. This committee brought together more than 130 voluntary groups to work in a more coordinated fashion. The national headquarters took on the responsibility for fundraising while relief delivery was decentralized to local groups. By 2002 the committee was able to raise 114,213 million *won*, which was redistributed through 435 projects to 2.91 million jobless people.[89]

New forms of inter-sector cooperation aimed to create straighter lines of authority between the state and voluntary agencies and to end the government's long involvement in private money mobilization. The rationale behind the Community Chest of Korea was to guarantee civil society's direct management of voluntary charities. The Kim Dae Jung government agreed with the need for a more transparent culture of fundraising and supported the launch of the Community Chest as a state–society partnership. However, and notwithstanding its endorsement of civic autonomy, the Community Chest in practice failed to achieve independence. Sixty percent of the fund was distributed to service proposals designed by the Ministry of Health and Welfare. Voluntary agencies had to share the remaining 40 percent, and the government introduced a new tool of control for its distribution, that of competitive bidding. In the 1999 allocation, only 149 out of 625 potential projects survived.[90] State interference in the composition of the board of trustees—by appointing the First Lady to the honorary chair and the former prime minister to the chair—discredited the trusteeship as a "rubber stamp board" acting on behalf of the government. Also, the Community Chest Law required the Community Chest to work in tandem with the government by stipulating that all of its voluntary activities should report to the Ministry of Health and Welfare. The voluntary sector was more than previously able to assert itself and to engage in more balanced partnerships with the state, but on the state side old habits lingered of wanting to see voluntarism as a tool of its will.

STATE STRATEGIES

In the previous chapter, we explored the symbiosis of state and business, cemented in part by social insurance. In the present chapter, we see how a parallel symbiosis emerged of state and voluntarism, cemented by social services. In the next chapter, we will explore in more detail how this legacy carried on into the democratic period. But before that, we will make use of the unexpected collaboration of authoritarianism and voluntarism to get more deeply into just what kind of legacy was created. Why did the state work in symbiosis with non-state actors, even allowing them space that was no doubt distasteful to authoritarian minds, such as that of General Park? How did they do it; how did they mobilize non-state actors for their purpose? And to what effect—what kind of mixed governance was created in this peculiar and uniquely Korean meeting ground of state and society?

Why?

The state used non-state actors for economic reasons. It needed to provide social insurance and it needed to get social services delivered, but it was determined to use its own budgets and administrative resources for economic development. It could not ignore social policy but needed others to do its bidding.

That is an important part of the explanation but not the whole explanation. There was more to it. There was an underlying vision of social cohesion. The authoritarian rulers saw themselves to be rescuing Korea from chaos and to be imposing order. The meaning of order they defined, but they were determined that it should be inclusive in the sense that all forces should contribute. Their vision for Korea was a typically *corporatist* one. The core of corporatist ideology is a blurring of the boundaries between state and civil society. Civil institutions merge with the state and lose their separate identities. The destruction of civil society is what primitive totalitarians resort to. Corporatists are more ambitious. They want all forces to contribute and pull together. They want conflict eliminated but not institutions; they just want all institutions to do as they should under the imperative of a necessary destiny. Historically, corporatism has been used as an institutional device to integrate conflicting social actors into a compromised synthesis.[91] Shifting welfare responsibilities onto the voluntary sector was not only a way of getting the job done cheaply, but also of deflecting civil society away from destructive egotism and mobilizing its institutions, with others, into the grand, shared, common national project of modernization.

Under the Park regime, the corporatist idea of social cohesion was manifested in the rallying of society in a spirit of sacrifice on behalf of the state's vision and leadership, be it the rallying of voluntary agencies for good works or the rallying of communities for self-help. The advent of the *Yushin* regime in the early 1970s led to a further intensification of state–corporatist ideas, crystallized into the *Saemaul* Movement. Through this campaign of mass mobilization, the regime assigned the main responsibility for community development to the villagers and local voluntary groups by emphasizing "assiduity," "self-help," and "cooperation." The ideological campaigning culminated in Park's 1974 New Year Address in which "the October *Yushin* is *Saemaul* Movement and *Saemaul* Movement is the October *Yushin*."[92] This powerful ideological drive by the authoritarian state served to sanctify state intervention into society and to integrate voluntary agencies as a key instrument of the state. The result was both successful mobilization and minimization of state expenditures.

The second military usurpation of power in 1980 again burdened the regime with the old problem of legitimacy. Together with social purification and economic stabilization, the idea of a new welfare state was brought to the fore. But despite its rhetoric of "welfare state" and state responsibility for welfare, the practical orientation was, as ever, "economy first." On welfare responsibilities, President Chun was blunt:

"In the societal field, welfare would be improved so tremendously that every individual would physically notice... The majority of the people may have felt already that economic stability is the very core of welfare. But, when we enter an advanced stage, the speed of that development would be further accelerated... We must pursue growth, but we must not repeat the mistake of letting growth stand in the way of welfare, a mistake we made in the 1970s. Nor should we follow the Western social security system which may be called anti-welfare as it has resulted in bringing growth to a standstill and high jobless rates. A system of welfare that is both mistake-proof and suited to our realities, I think, should be based on stable economic growth and equal job opportunities for all the people."[93]

Criticizing not only the previous regime's excesses but also government-led welfare failure in the West, the Chun government was innovative more in terminology than in action. Its "welfare state'" was mainly old wine in new bottles. Social policy was to remain an integral part of economic policy and selective provision to stay in the hands of non-state actors, including voluntary associations.

In the period of re-democratization, boundaries between the state and civil society were redefined in that civil institutions asserted their autonomy, but the corporate legacy lingered. The Roh government responded to social demands by appealing to "citizens from all walks of life to tighten their belts and work even harder" to enhance the productivity of the economy and stressed the important roles of individuals, families, and communities in providing social services.[94] The priority of economic predominance over social concerns was set in stone, and social service delivery continued to be outsourced to voluntary agencies. Even the Kim Young Sam government, which took pride in being a civilian government, duplicated the economy-centered orientation of public policy and took refuge in the established social reliance on the voluntary sector. The 1994 declaration of "globalization strategy" as a key policy orientation of the administration defined increased international competitiveness as a national priority that was to inform all state policies including social policy.[95] Through the Presidential Committee on the Globalization Campaign as of 1995, the government sketched a "New Korean Welfare Model" based on five principles grounded in neo-liberal values, including the diversification-of-service-provider principle, which reiterated the state's continued reliance on the voluntary sector in the localization of welfare responsibility.[96] The Committee stressed "welfare partnerships" and embraced voluntary groups as qualified partners for the government.

Integrated economic and social policy was again the grounding idea in the aftermath of the financial crisis, now in the language of "productive welfare" as articulated by Kim Dae Jung. President Kim's vision of a new constructive system of welfare, laid out in a Liberation Day speech on August 15, 1999, rested on post-crisis institutional reform and an assumption that the economy would ride out the crisis so that governance could be directed to welfare issues and the social inclusion of displaced workers and families. The idea was again a corporatist one of social harmony, now between democratic, market, and social forces.[97] The Kim administration was keen to develop a Korean version of what in Europe was thought of as "the third way," seeking to incorporate both neo-liberal economic principles and democratic commitments to social justice.[98] Productive welfare was seen as a positive-sum combination of economic growth and the augmentation of social protection and converged into strengthening yet further the role of civic groups and voluntary associations.[99]

How?

In its mobilization and control of the voluntary sector, the state has continuously relied on a combination of legal and institutional strategies to tie voluntarism down with social accountability for service provision.

In authoritarian and democratic periods alike, the common feature of legislation has been to specify the mixed responsibility of state and non-state entities, primarily individuals, families, and voluntary associations, rather than of the state alone. The state has enabled itself to both claim ownership of social responsiveness and to pass the buck of practical responsibility on to others. That division of labor was modified after 1997, but not suspended.

Throughout the 1950s, the predominance of foreign voluntary agencies in the terrain of emergency relief drove the Rhee government to perceive the voluntary sector as a potential challenge to its authority and to enact a series of regulations for the controlled mobilization of foreign relief as a replacement for state welfare. The first step was to impose a duty of registration on foreign agencies. In August 1953, the government imposed a Memorandum on Relief Supplies in order to control the inflow of foreign voluntary resources. Foreign agencies had to register with both Korean and UN authorities in order to operate, including for duty-free import of relief supplies. The duty of registration soon passed exclusively to Korean authorities. As of 1955 foreign agencies were obliged to report regularly on their activities to the Ministry of Health and Social Affairs, to appear at the Ministry when called upon, and to receive advice or cautions about the directions of their work. Through these devices, the government was to some degree able to direct and redirect the efforts of foreign agencies, for example in response to natural disasters or other emergencies.

The Park regime brought in a stronger regulatory framework in the 1963 Foreign Voluntary Relief Agencies Act, which stipulated a standard definition of foreign voluntary agencies and controlled their relief activities in a systematic fashion. With the pretext of facilitating the communication with foreign voluntary agencies, the military junta established national and regional Relief Coordination Committees and dispatched an army of officials to serve them, and thereby brought their supervision into the institutional chain of command.[100] Foreign voluntary agencies were now required to present quarterly work plans three months in advance, while the Ministry of Health and Social Affairs took to allocating specific tasks to individual agencies. In 1970 followed the Social Welfare Service Act, the thrust of which was to impose more specific duties of social service delivery on the voluntary sector or other non-governmental actors.

Under the rosy rhetoric of the construction of the welfare state, the Chun regime proactively passed a series of social welfare acts in response to its legitimacy deficits and the growing influence of voluntary associations. The Elderly Welfare Act was passed in 1981 and revised in 1984, the Law for the Education of Preschool Children in 1982, the Disability Welfare Act in 1981 and revised in 1984, the Child Welfare Act in 1981 and revised in 1984, and the Mother and Child Health Act as a supplementation to the Child Welfare Act in 1986. Indeed, it was not until Chun's authoritarian regime that the tri-polar structure of social welfare services—children, the elderly, and the disabled—was completed by legal measures articulating operational guidelines that social welfare corporations or other voluntary welfare associations had to follow. The Social Welfare Service Act was revised in 1983 to lay down with yet more clarity the responsibilities of voluntary actors in operating social welfare corporations and facilities.

The democratic transition in the late 1980s and the financial crisis in the late 1990s triggered new legislation on the state–voluntarism corporatist accommodation. From 1989 to 2002, more than 40 new acts or major revisions of existing acts pertaining to social services were passed. The Kim Dae Jung government launched a Regulatory Reform Planning Board in May 1998, designed to streamline the inclusion of voluntary forces into integrated welfare schemes. The Nonprofit and Voluntary Organizations Assistance Act of 2000 introduced both subsidies and concessions on taxation and postal fees in return for increased voluntary participation in public welfare programs. Voluntary agencies had in theory become free agents, but in practice their state dependency continued. The scarcity of private financial resources contributed to locking the voluntary sector in institutional shackles of enforced compliance with the Nonprofit and Voluntary Organizations Assistance Act and its related conditions.

The primary channel of institutional influence under the Park regime was in the field of financial mobilization, which was put under the control of quasi-government, quasi-voluntary corporations. The Disaster Relief Act in 1962 established a government-sponsored nonprofit corporation, the National Association for Disaster Relief, for the purpose of collecting the Disaster Relief

Fund in lieu of the government. In 1974, the Ministry of Home Affairs set up another pro-government corporation for the Help-Your-Neighbor-Fund, which was used as a source of assistance for people in need.

In the Social Welfare Service Funds Act in December 1980, the Chun regime further encouraged private financial mobilization, resulting in the National Association for Disaster Relief dramatically increasing the Disaster Relief Fund to over 40 times the amount of previous collections. In close cooperation with the government, an average of 300 million *won* was distributed annually through the Disaster Relief Fund to flood victims and people afflicted by other natural disasters.[101]

The government also appropriated portions of the Disaster Relief Fund and Help-Your-Neighbor-Fund for its own public assistance schemes. The funds were kept and managed by the Bank of Korea in close coordination with the Ministry of Health and Social Affairs. This enabled a share of the annual surplus and interest to be siphoned off for government welfare programs. In 1981, the Bank of Korea integrated both funds into a joint "Fund for Social Welfare Programs," thereby strengthening its control over the whole process of financial transfers of voluntary donations. It was not until the enactment of the 1997 Community Chest Law that the voluntary sector was in principle given legal entitlement over the use of the funds it itself collected, and even that, as we have seen, was more a formality than a reality.

The Chun regime's institutional design for voluntary welfare activities came in the form of co-optation through "participation," in effect a form of institutional manipulation in the sense that the underlying objective was less to empower participants in the process of planning and decision making than to enable the government to incorporate, selectively, a limited number of key voluntary agencies.[102] The government promoted integrated delivery as a key principle of the Fifth Economic and Social Development Plan.[103] Criticizing the lack of coordination between service providers during the Park regime, the government now stressed inter-sector cooperation and the active participation of key voluntary associations in the integrated delivery system. This co-optation was intended to secure the strategic regulation of large national voluntary associations, with the aim of diluting welfare demands and holding down public welfare expenditures. Subsequent governments, even after the democratic transition, continued the use of institutional arrangements of co-optation, albeit with varying degrees of scale and strength.

During the democratic transition, and in the face of an upsurge of assertive civic groups, the state's institutional adaptations became more subtle and sophisticated. The tradition of state provision via voluntary agencies persisted, now resting on a manipulation of the internal bifurcation in the voluntary sector between conventional and new networks. By differentiating the intensity of accommodation, the state kept incorporating voluntary agencies both as facilitators of service delivery and as social partners in cushioning the pressure for welfare reform.

The politicization of new voluntary networks was handled by mainly symbolic institutional reform. A first move toward reactive accommodation after the 1987 June Uprising came through new directives on social work, in reality makeshift initiatives to forestall real reform. The Roh government was not about to upgrade the status of social workers from contract-based low-rank staff to full-time and better salaried workers. In 1995, the Kim Young Sam government even suspended the recruitment of new social workers for financial reasons. The same year, it launched the Presidential Committee on Public Administrative Reforms, where the general direction of bureaucratic reform was discussed with, again, selected voluntary advocacy groups. These post-democratization governments perfected the habit of bringing key welfare groups into institutions of social policy decision making—for instance, the Welfare Policy Committee for the Disabled in 1988, the Welfare Policy Committee for the Elderly in 1991, and the Consultation Committee on Social Security in 1995. In a continuation of established techniques, the Kim Young Sam government exploited internal voluntary sector divisions by turning to *conventional* welfare organizations as priority partners for the delivery of welfare services and the mobilization of financial resources for self-sufficiency and awarding selected agencies favorable treatment and support.[104]

After the financial crisis, the Kim Dae Jung government defined itself as a risk controller and social integrator by advancing "productive welfare" as an institutional device to combine neo-liberal activation with the reinforcement of social safety nets. The National Basic Livelihood Security extended social protection within a welfare-to-work paradigm and made the state more of a provider.[105] A group of scholars go so far as to argue that the Korean welfare regime in the post-crisis years thereby established the foundations of a fully fledged modern welfare state, even moving toward a Scandinavian-type welfare regime.[106] However, such an assertion ignores counterfactual evidence in two ways. First, Korea's public social expenditure, despite increasing after the crisis (from 3.80 percent of the GDP in 1997 to 5.15 percent in 1998), still ranks as the lowest among the OECD countries. Further, the Kim Dae Jung government put relatively little emphasis on social services as compared to public assistance. The share of the Ministry of Health and Welfare budget to social welfare services in fact declined after the 1997 crisis. The state continued its outsourcing of service provision to the third sector and the state–voluntarism partnerships remained a critical component also of Kim's productive welfare.

MODES OF MIXED GOVERNANCE

When we observe the Korean state through the prism of the voluntary sector, we see in clear relief what we in Chapter 2 have called "mixed governance" and how this has been a constant characteristic of the Korean state. However, although a constant, it has not been an unchanging constant. Through shifting regimes, the voluntary sector has been both collaborator and challenger, but in different periods more of one and less of the other. The state has constantly, and with sophistication, co-opted voluntary actors and integrated them into its design, but again in different ways depending on changing contexts. Mixed governance has come about through the state's legislative and institutional regulation of non-state actors. The weight of state regulation has been shifting, depending on the capacity of non-state actors to influence state policies and to stand up against state pressures and, in the case of the state–voluntarism welfare mix, the balance of power between hard state and soft voluntarism. The Korean welfare mix can be classified in four different modes of equilibrium defined by shifting patterns of (1) state guidance, (2) financing, and (3) service delivery.

Foreign Agency-Based Welfare Mix

The first pattern of the welfare mix is between foreign agencies and the war-stricken state of the Rhee government in the 1950s. The supremacy in governance was emergency relief, and this became the initial remit of foreign voluntarism. Relief activities were mostly both financed and implemented by foreign agencies with little or no institutional backup from the Korean state. However, the direction of voluntary action was nevertheless to some degree guided and regulated by the state in, for example, mandatory registration and reporting and in an imposed readiness to comply with state-defined priorities. The state's legal restrictions on foreign relief activities—such as the mandatory requirements of registration and reports and the readiness for additional tasks requested by the government—did curtail the autonomy of the voluntary agencies and coerced their financing and service delivery into becoming compatible with the broad directions of state policies.

On the other hand, public services in this period were extremely residual and selective. The Rhee government relied upon the outdated *Chosŏn* Poor Law left over from the Japanese colonial government as its main instrument of social policy and did not introduce new measures except in a limited way for military and police personnel and war veterans, and only in 1959 for selected civil servants. The state, with no capacity of its own of either finance or delivery and dependent on foreign assistance, could guide but not coerce, and foreign agencies, effectively replacing the state in the provision of social services, could operate with relative impunity.

State-Imposed Welfare Mix

In the authoritarian period, the government continued to rely on voluntary agencies but also took control. Foreign voluntarism was phased out and replaced by indigenous agencies. Guidance was strengthened in the direction of command. Finance continued to be mainly from outside of state budgets and provision in the hands of non-state actors, but again under more firm state control.

Voluntarism in this period was merged into a larger corporatist design under a powerful logic of "self-reliance." This was a state-imposed welfare mix of mobilization: voluntarism was mobilized by legislation and communities and eventually workplaces by the ideological trappings of the *Saemaul* Movement.

The Park regime used mass campaigns to mobilize individuals, families, villages, and workers to improve living conditions through efforts of their own and without direct government engagement, in particular in financial terms. In 1972, 28 billion *won* worth of labor and financial resources—89.5 percent of the total *Saemaul* investment—was provided by local villagers themselves. State-provided financial support did not reach the level of that provided by local communities themselves until 1975, and even at its peak did not account for more than about half of the total investment, the state then achieving a roughly 200 percent return on its outlays. Contrary to the government propaganda that its concentrated efforts to increase public financing made it possible for rural communities to improve household incomes, the main financial contributions for rural development had been mobilized from individual household budgets. In fact, the role of the state was mostly confined to being a regulator or usher of the *Saemaul* Movement, whereas local communities played multiple roles in financing, management, and implementation.

The state's efforts to capitalize on the *Saemaul* Movement culminated in the dispatch throughout the country of *Saemaul* leaders. People with various social backgrounds were selected and trained by the Ministry of Home Affairs and its related public interest corporations for the mission of supervising community development projects.[107]

Quasi-public voluntary corporations were established as engines for the mobilization of voluntary resources. The National Council of *Saemaul* Movement played an intermediate role between the government and local communities, acting as a vanguard and agent of the government's mission and policy. Various *Saemaul*-related quasi-governmental corporations were established and lined up under the National Council's coordination: the Central Association of Rural Leaders in 1971, the Central Association of *Saemaul* Women Leaders in 1980, the Central Association of *Saemaul* Leaders in 1980, the Central Association of Factory *Saemaul* Movement in 1980, and the Central Association of *Saemaul* Young Leaders in 1981.

This hierarchical structure of the strong state, quasi-voluntary corporations and local community groups constituted, it could be argued, a successful case of cooperation but is probably more fittingly seen, following Durkheim, as a "forced division of labor" in which the voluntary sector was involuntarily obliged to undertake the task that was imposed on it by the state.[108] In this division of labor, the voluntary sector and community-based groups served as extended arms of the state, and the state effectively laid welfare responsibilities on voluntary agencies, religious charities, and families.

Integrated Welfare Mix

The most catholic pattern of the mixed economy of welfare in modern Korea is the "integrated welfare mix"—grounded in the premise that voluntary welfare production is integrated in the overall welfare design of the state but also that voluntary agencies are in some measure partners of the state and not just its servants. The two main forms are "integrated autonomy" and "integrated dependence."[109]

The former can be interpreted as an ideal of democratic pluralism in the sense that groups of people organize to impact upon public policies which affect them, but without becoming trapped and bound into decision making or implementation processes. New voluntary associations that emerged as political advocacy groups sought to define their relations to the state in this way. The state, however, responded by co-opting some peak associations from among the new social groups into government-led consultation institutions under a guise of state–society partnerships, thereby undermining their autonomy of advocacy.

In integrated dependence, on the other hand, voluntary agencies are pulled into partnerships in which they are made financially and otherwise dependent on the government. This was the lot of many conventional voluntary associations from the 1980s and onward.

In the long process of democratization, when civil society groups were gradually able to assert themselves more strongly, the state-imposed welfare mix was superseded and replaced by a more integrated model. The character of that new equilibrium, however, was and has remained, democracy notwithstanding, decidedly in the direction of integrated dependence. During re-democratization in the period after 1987, the governments were forced into civil society partnerships but worked to frame those partnerships so as to neutralize advocacy autonomy. The habit of co-optation lingered in the welfare-to-work programs linked to the National Basic Livelihood Security in the aftermath of the financial crisis.[110] This welfare mix blurred the traditional boundary between social welfare services and public assistance. The task of running self-support aid programs supplementing the National Basic Livelihood Security was assigned primarily to voluntary welfare organizations and community groups in coordination with the Ministry of Health and Welfare or local governments. In particular, voluntary groups in local communities contributed to cultivating self-help-to-work initiatives designed to improve basic work or entrepreneurial skills of participants. The participation of the voluntary sector in self-help aid programs expanded its range of activity from mainly services to including also public assistance.

One product of the transition from a state-imposed to an integrated welfare mix was to lift the voluntary sector out of the ghetto of service provision to which it had been confined and had confined itself and into a broader range of social policy provision.

Competition-Based Welfare Mix

In a competitive welfare mix, the state is first "rule-setter" and then provider of public finance via contract-based competition. The voluntary sector, as a "rule-taker," needs to customize itself to the requirements of the state if it wants to obtain finance and contracts. The voluntary sector must accept the logic of explicit competition but is in return relieved of some burdens of fundraising.

The state–voluntarism welfare mix in Korea started to be taken in a competitive direction with the Nonprofit and Voluntary Organizations Aid Project, which was launched in 1999 under the Ministry of Government Administration and Home Affairs. This was a project to distribute public funds to promote grass-roots participatory democracy and to use the voluntary sector to provide services in unexplored areas that the bureaucratic outreach could not cover.[111] In 2002, the Ministry defined eight different clusters of relevant activity. Judged by accepted proposals, its priority turned out to be "social integration," meaning provisions for the new poor in the post-crisis society.

The setting up of quasi-market schemes in a competition-based welfare mix comes, as Ralf Dahrendorf has warned, with costs to the voluntary sector.[112] Contract arrangements formalized a collaborative but divided structure between voluntary agencies. The state's preservation of its control over finances and rules of operation served to encourage a culture of clientelism that discouraged independent fundraising and fostered pro-government biases within the voluntary sector itself. While the number of association that applied for state-funded projects decreased, the number of projects accepted by the Ministry increased. Hence, the more contracting, the less participation by the voluntary sector and the more fidelity by the remaining groups. The introduction of competitiveness thereby served to reinforce the tendency toward integrated dependence in state–voluntary relations, although many voluntary associations opted for non-participation as it became clear that participation came at the price of sacrificing the very principle of voluntarism.

Nevertheless, the state derived benefits from the manipulations of the Nonprofit and Voluntary Organizations Aid Projects. It was able to identify who would be pro-governmental voluntary associations, winnow them from the others, and channel them to leadership roles in the non-state branch of the new post-crisis Korean welfare state.

PERSISTENT CORPORATISM

We should now be starting to get a firmer grip on the enigmatic Korean state. The seeds of strong statism were sown during the First Republic and perfected during authoritarianism. The resulting unequivocally strong state turned to governing by putting society under control, in periods under brutal control, in its determination to hold on to power, but, strangely enough, not under command in its determination to use power. Rather, it governed by mobilizing economic and social forces into a modernization project of its own definition.

While still underdeveloped, Korea was, as are underdeveloped countries generally, "invaded" by an army of what is today called NGOs. That is often a mixed blessing. Many developing countries experience that while NGOs bring capacities to the host country, they also to some degree take over and come to stand in the way of the building up of national administrative capacities.[113] That did not happen in Korea, where foreign voluntarism was rapidly transformed into an indigenous capacity.

The voluntary sector takes us deeper into the state–society relationship than we have been able to penetrate so far. The dictators took what they were given and ran with it. They took the state and turned it into an awesome force for their purpose. They reluctantly took the emerging corporate capitalism and gave it marching orders. They took Confucian social life and energized it by mass mobilization. They took the American legacy of voluntarism and made it Korean. And, more than that, they turned all of this into a *system*. State, capital, labor, mass mobilization, and voluntarism were made to reinforce each other and to pull together. It was not done nicely, but it was done systematically and to great effect.

Mixed governance was a necessity. The state was strong but could not forge its intended development without the contribution of non-state actors, a contribution it had to make them want to provide. But it also represented a vision of corporatist social cohesion. The precise shape of mixed governance has fluctuated, but the corporatist system has persisted. That system, on the one hand, made Korea a society rich in institutions, and that again was to help the country in its re-transition into democracy. On the other hand, corporatism became entrenched and persisted into democratic consolidation. When Kim Dae Jung at the moment of victory, for himself and for democracy, was challenged by economic crisis, it was the corporatist legacy he could reach back to for the redesigning of industrial relations and state policies.

5

THE STATE MEETS DEMOCRACY

When President Chun Doo Hwan's term in office approached its end in 1987, it became visible again that Korea was a democracy in which democratic government had been suspended. The attempt by the ruling elite to preserve the autocratic order provoked the June Uprising, with nationwide demonstrations with direct and violent confrontations between demonstrators and police in most cities across the country. Confrontation was nothing new to the Korean dictators, but this time it proved impossible to contain the uprising. The ruling Democratic Justice Party conceded on constitutional reform, and the main political parties could agree on a new constitution in which elections would be direct and properly democratic. That put an end to the intense confrontations between the authoritarian regime and the pro-democracy movements, and the Fifth Republic gave in.

The elections in December were, however, a democratic setback in that Roh Tae Woo, the candidate of the authoritarian establishment, was elected. The opposition was hopelessly divided and Roh took the presidency with only 36.6 percent of the vote. The break with the authoritarian past was only partial, and it was to be another 10 years before democracy would be consolidated.

THE STATE

From 1987 to 1997, the Korean state metamorphosed from authoritarianism to democracy. The presidency changed, although it has remained the central institution in the state system. The political machinery through which the president worked changed, and the role of the National Assembly and of political parties changed. Forces from below were legitimized and started to be given normal participation in politics and planning. This all happened gradually and hesitantly, but by the time Kim Dae Jung took office in 1998, the old authoritarian elite had finally been seen off and a reformed state stood ready to work democratically.

The Presidency

Although democratized, the constitution of the Sixth Republic retained the strong presidency. The president appoints the prime minister and cabinet and directs executive and advisory agencies. The Office of the President, the Blue House, continued to enjoy its superior status in central decision making and management.

Both President Roh Tae Woo and President Kim Young Sam were Korean conservatives. Roh had been a co-conspirator with Chun Doo Hwan in the 1979 coup and the number-two man during Chun's presidency. Although Kim was an erstwhile opponent of military authoritarianism, his power base as president was in the 1990 "Grand Conservative Coalition" of Roh's ruling conservative party, another conservative party headed by Kim Chong-p'il, and his own party, which he had brought out of opposition, seeing a conservative coalition as his best opportunity of becoming president. Under these two presidents, the old conservative elite and their partners in big business continued to dominate political life.

Also intact was the structure of ministries. The Blue House was in command, economy-related ministries led, and other ministries were subordinate. What eventually did change, however, was the role of local government. Local self-governance had been a constitutional aspiration already in the First Republic but was not implemented and subsequently held back during the authoritarian period. However, the June 29 declaration of 1987 included provisions for local self-government through popular elections of local assemblies and heads of local governments. The Local Autonomy Election Act was passed in 1988 but first vetoed by President Roh and only promulgated in 1989 after negotiations between the ruling and opposition parties. Local assembly elections took place in 1991, but the Roh government delayed the elections of local government heads until 1995. Local governments would wield considerable authority, including in taxation, but also work under the pressure of financial and administrative controls from the central government.

During the authoritarian regime, the state intelligence agency (the Korea Central Intelligence Agency, from 1981 the National Security Planning Agency) was used by presidents as a powerful tool of control and terror. With democratization, that power was reined in, in particular in domestic political surveillance. Under President Kim Dae Jung, the agency became the National Intelligence

Service and had its mandate specified to gathering data on counterterrorism and international matters.

Advisory Agencies

The novelty in the underlying structure of advisory agencies was the emergence of advisory and negotiating institutions with proper union representation. This happened gradually and hesitantly, first in the form of consultative bodies with representatives of workers, employers, and public interest groups, such as the Minimum Wage Council, established in 1987, and the National Economic and Social Council, set up in 1990 following an initiative from the moderate Federation of Korean Trade Unions. These bodies broadened the landscape of social dialogue, but in a limited way. The government did not participate directly, and the emerging independent trade union movement was excluded. In May 1996, the Industrial Relations Reform Commission was appointed as a presidential advisory body. For the first time, independent trade unions were included, although still not officially legal. The hope had been that the commission would find its way to consensus on labor law reform, but that failed in a way that produced a mini political crisis that helped toward democratic consolidation. More on this follows below.

What became known as the Tripartite Commission (in Korean, the Labor-Management-Government Commission) was appointed as an initiative of President-elect Kim Dae Jung before he took office.[114] This was the definitive opening of institutional channels of trade union participation in the making of public policy and marked the ending of the old bipartite government–business coalition. Although the commission faced a number of problems and obstacles, it proved an effective venue of interaction between forces from above and from below that had previously been held institutionally apart. It was instrumental in hammering out a historic social compromise in February 1998 that paved the way for decisive changes in the structure of social policy and governance.

Other inclusive advisory agencies followed—for example, the Presidential Committee on Policy Planning and the Presidential Committee on Quality of Life. The purpose of tripartite and other broadly based consultative institutions was to tie social partners into a cooperative process of breathing life into vague presidential ideas for the direction of public policy, such as the "juxtaposed development of democracy and the market economy" and "productive welfare."

The National Assembly and Political Parties

With re-democratization, Korea's unicameral National Assembly regained the powers it had lost under the authoritarian regimes, and the executive became normally dependent on the legislature's consent. In the first years of the Roh government, when opposition parties enjoyed a majority in the National Assembly, the legislature held strong sway in policy making. However, when the

Grand Conservative Coalition was formed in 1990, the National Assembly lost clout and was once more dominated by the executive.

Revitalized political parties became regionally based. One of Park Chung Hee's strategic mistakes had been to engineer a geographically inequitable distribution of economic resources. This resulted in an uneven regional development that was to be a constant source of political discontent and unrest and eventually contributed to undermining the authoritarian regime. The southeast province of *Kyŏngsang*, for example, the home region of several of the authoritarian leaders, had benefitted at the expense of the southwest province of *Chŏlla*, Kim Dae Jung's home region and political base. Kwangju, a major city in the *Chŏlla* province, had been the site of fierce anti-authoritarian demonstrations in 1980, known as the Kwangju Uprising, which were brutally and ruthlessly repressed by the coup forces. Kim Young Sam had his political base in the *Kyŏngsang* region. The Grand Conservative Coalition not only left Kim Dae Jung politically isolated but also continued the alienation of the *Chŏlla* region. These two Kims, once allies in opposition, became intense rivals for the presidency, and regionalism was a decisive factor in presidential elections in 1987, 1992, and 1997.

In parliamentary elections, regionalism was reinforced by a first-past-the-post electoral system in small, single-member constituencies. For instance, in the 2000 National Assembly elections, the main conservative party based in the *Kyŏngsang* region captured all but one of 65 seats in this region, while the *Chŏlla*-based party led by Kim Dae Jung failed to win a single seat in spite of polling on average 13 percent of the vote. Regionalism thus became a serious institutional barrier to "the deepening of democracy, not only by reducing political accountability and policy-based competition between parties within national politics, but also by dividing the various groups and social classes of civil society against their own common interest."[115]

Prior to 1997, there was little substantive difference between the parties in ideology, policy, or organizational structures.[116] The main political parties were not ideologically based. They were frequently dissolved and merged to satisfy the ambitions of political leaders or factional bosses. Intra-party democracy was underdeveloped and leadership oligarchic. Smaller progressive, labor, or opposition groups were disadvantaged by the electoral system. Up to the 2004 parliamentary elections, there was no labor or left-leaning party representation in the National Assembly.[117]

The election of President Kim Dae Jung marked the first transition of power from the conservative elite (the Grand National Party) to an opposition force (the National Congress for New Politics) since the establishment of the Republic of Korea in 1948. It was also the first electoral victory of the *Chŏlla* political camp. In order to win, however, Kim Dae Jung had to enter into an alliance with the conservative United Liberal Democrats headed by Kim Chong-p'il and formed a de facto coalition government. The National Assembly was still dominated by the conservative coalition, which won both the 1996 and 2000 parliamentary elections and denied Kim Dae Jung's alliance a majority in the Assembly.

Forces from Below

The events of 1987 were massively significant. The constitution was democratized, the National Assembly reassumed normal powers, basic civil rights were restored, freedom of the press was re-established, and local autonomy was revived. But it was still democracy with limitations. The authoritarian legacy lingered. Civil society was able to assert itself freely and legally, but within persisting constraints. State–society relations remained uneasy and unsettled for another 10 years.

The labor movement remained weak, divided against itself, and enjoyed limited respect and authority in the broader society. Union militancy continued to be heavily firm-based. It would take 10 years and a direct confrontation with the lingering authoritarian tendency for unions to be able to claim normal democratic recognition.

During the "Great Labor Struggle" of July and August 1987, more than 1,200 new unions were organized. Particularly conspicuous was the formation of white-collar unions. A new national organization of trade unions was formed, the progressive Korean Confederation of Trade Unions (KCTU), explicitly against and in competition with the existing and more or less discredited but still privileged Federation of Korean Trade Unions (FKTU).

The old labor laws remained in effect and still prohibited multiple trade unions (and thereby the legal recognition of new unions that were formed independently of the FKTU), third-party intervention in collective bargaining, and political activity on the part of trade unions. Organized labor was widely seen as "a villain responsible for a multitude of economic ills, with a long series of government and mass media reports suggesting that the high wages of Korean workers were the chief culprits robbing the competitive edge of the Korean economy."[118] Government mindsets were fixed on global competitiveness through market liberalizations. Employers responded to the upsurge in union activity with numerous dismissals of trade union activists and a tougher line on back pay after strike action.[119] They were hostile to any change in labor relations except for increasing labor market flexibility.

In the run-up to joining the Organization of Economic Co-operation and Development (OECD) in 1996, Korea had taken on an obligation to bring labor legislation in line with advanced international standards. This caused the old conservative coalition to mobilize a last stance against a progressive reform of industrial relations. Employers, chaebŏl, a conservative National Assembly, government officials in economic ministries, and a weaker and more compliant president conspired for legislative reform less in favor of workers' rights and more for "flexibility."

The Kim Young Sam administration seemed to grow overconfident of its political capability. It deliberately delayed easing restrictions on union activity in spite of a commitment to the OECD to do so. In a hopelessly clumsy step after the failure of the Presidential Commission for Industrial Relations Reform, a majority of the National Assembly, not including opposition members, was convened in a secret session on the early morning of December 26 and clandestinely passed a pro-business and pro-labor-market-flexibility revision of the labor law. This predictably backfired. Civil society groups, especially trade unions, were outraged and launched nationwide protests for the immediate nullification of the new act. The KCTU, still not officially legalized, and the old FKTU for once joined forces and set in motion a series of strikes, including a successful general strike in January 1997. Moreover, the labor movement had public opinion on its side, and it simply transpired that the time had passed that a conservative elite could railroad through self-serving public policies in disregard of civil rights and public opinion.

On January 21, President Kim Young Sam met with the leaders of the main political parties in the National Assembly, and negotiations were started to rewrite the law. On March 10, the law passed in December was revised again to incorporate compromises between the ruling and opposition parties. Their revision gave labor only limited material concessions—but power relations had changed irreversibly.

The resulting structure of social representation was, however, quite complicated. Given regionalized politics, the existing major parties were unable to absorb and represent social divisions and effectively conceded this function to civic organizations, who were thereby able to contribute importantly to democratic vitality and to participate effectively in political processes.[120] These organizations, in turn, were politically divided. Despite authoritarian repression, there was a long tradition of radical and militant social movement in Korea, often referred to as "the people's movement," which had tended to pursue fundamental changes in the capitalist economy and class system. At least a part of the labor movement was aligned with this tradition. The radical organizations nevertheless failed to win decisive influence. Democratization had spawned a new generation of social movement, "the new citizens' movement," which differentiated itself from the radical movements by being oriented toward gradual institutional reform of unjust social and economic conditions within the capitalist system. Whereas the people's movement groups were predominantly grounded in the working class, the peasantry, the urban poor, and students, and militant and often violent in strategy, the new citizens' movement groups had their base in the middle class and among white-collar workers, professionals, religious leaders, and intellectuals, and were legalistic in strategy.[121] These organizations were politically successful throughout the 1990s. The most influential and representative groups were the Citizens' Coalition for Economic Justice, the Korean

Federation of Environmental Movement, and the People's Solidarity for Participatory Democracy. They were able to take on a role as "policy entrepreneurs," who were "willing to invest resources of various kinds in hopes of a future return in the form of policies they favor."[122] The important and innovative National Basic Livelihood Security Act grew in part out of the activism of pro-welfare organizations, which saw themselves to be representing the interests and rights of the poor.

Power relations had changed, but what emerged as a social base for Kim Dae Jung was still a limited coalition between a challenged democratic elite and a constellation of moderate, if not conservative, social movements.

NEW POLITICAL CONSTELLATIONS

As the structure of the state changed, so did the content of governance—eventually. And when it did, that happened only partially as a result of democratization. Kim Dae Jung came into office on the back of two upheavals. There was the slow and gradual process of democratization, which culminated with his election. And then there was the sudden and unexpected shock of the Asian economic crisis, which hit Korea at the very time he was fighting and winning the election. Economic growth was dented and seriously threatened, and large sections of the population suffered a decline in their standard of living, economic insecurity, and unemployment. The form that governance now took was therefore a result of two simultaneous and dramatic events: a great step forward politically and a great step backward economically.

Economic Crisis

In November 1997, with foreign exchange reserves dangerously low, the Korean government was forced to ask the International Monetary Fund (IMF) for help. The IMF responded with a package containing, on the one hand, an unprecedented USD$57 billion bailout, and on the other hand its standard package of neo-liberal structural adjustment and market liberalizations. The package was imposed on Korea—not only the president but also the three major competing presidential candidates were forced to sign the agreement—in a way that was widely seen to be embarrassing and humiliating, bordering on the forced surrender of independence. Embarrassment turned to anger directed at the *chaebŏl* that were seen to have behaved with financial irresponsibility and to have brought economic mayhem to the nation.

The origins of the crisis are a matter of controversy. One school attributes it mainly to domestic peculiarities in the Korean model, which generated crony capitalism, corruption, and excessive debt.[123] Others put the blame on external factors, such as the post-cold-war dismantling of an Asian model, especially the traditional mechanisms of generating and coordinating long-term investments, under American patronage and the liberalization of financial markets through-out the region.[124] "Beginning with a run on Thailand's currency in the early summer, the contagion spread through one Asian economy after another, until it struck Korea like a force-10 typhoon in November, (leaving) the economy essen-tially bankrupt."[125]

Economic performance collapsed from a positive real GDP growth rate of 5 percent in 1997 to a negative rate of nearly 7 percent in 1998. Unemployment increased from 2.6 percent of the workforce in 1997 to 5.6 percent in the first quarter of 1998, and then peaked at 8.4 percent in the first quarter of 1999. The number of unemployed exceeded 1 million in the first quarter of 1998, and peaked at 1.75 million in 1999.

Reform

Now followed what in the Korean context was serious reform on three levels: labor market reform, *chaebŏl* reform, and, crucially for the present narrative, welfare reform.

Welfare reform was not inevitable. Other countries in the region, such as Hong Kong and Singapore, weathered the crisis without it. The catalyst in Korea was democratic consolidation. The dual influence of economic and political factors played out in the following way. The crisis generated problems that, given democratic consolidation, would have to be responded to and made it imperative and obvious that there would be some kind of reshaping of govern-ment approaches and programs. Given the minimal role of state welfare and a strong emphasis on self-reliance, there were insufficient public provisions for the new unemployed in a country that had maintained near-full employment prior to the economic crisis. Family support and occupational welfare, which had obviated much of the need for state welfare, could hardly exert their protective role against the backdrop of the economic crisis. Even the IMF bailout package emphasized the need for better social safety nets.

It was, however, political dynamics more than economic necessity that was to decide the direction of reform. Rather than the social role of the state being contracted, as might have been expected for economic reasons, it was in fact radically extended, both quantitatively and qualitatively. That is explained, firstly, by the new strength of forces from below and the new power they could muster behind the reforms they had long been advocating, and, secondly and decisively, by how stronger forces from below and new forces from above joined in inter-preting the crisis and how they interacted to forge the public policy response that was to follow. A more progressive regime came to power and was able to use pressure from below as leverage to benefit from a window of opportunity that opened when the economic crisis temporarily weakened the resistance of the otherwise-still-strong conservative coalition.

The outcome was a step change in the social role of the state. The Korean welfare state has continued to work as a regulatory state, but now took on, in addition, an extended role as a provider state. This was the first real discontinuity in welfare state developments since the launch of compulsory social insurance with industrial accident insurance in 1963. The state changed, becoming democratic, and the welfare state changed, taking on a qualitatively new kind of provider responsibility.

President Kim offered Korea a new paradigm of "productive welfare." His Committee for Quality of Life defined that lofty slogan to comprise three aspects: (a) distribution through the establishment of a fair and orderly market (welfare in terms of participation in the production process); (b) redistribution by state welfare (welfare for securing the basic livelihood); and (c) social investment in self-support (welfare to provide self-support aid to the underprivileged).[126] The Presidential Commission on Policy Planning proposed three key principles: (a) guaranteeing a minimum standard of living for those without the ability to work; (b) supporting self-reliance and self-support by virtue of the centrality of work and human capital development; and (c) more efficiently and democratically managing welfare institutions by increasing the involvement of local authorities, the private sector, and the community in policy design and implementation.[127]

Much was to be the same then—in particular the mixed economy of welfare. The responsibilities of individuals and families were, as always, the base. Welfare remained work-oriented, and "productive welfare" imported into the Korean model the Western currency of workfare and welfare to work. But there was also a decisive novelty: the guarantee (in principle) by the state of a social minimum.

The first step was a linked labor market and unemployment reform whereby labor market "flexibility" was made palatable on the promise of better unemployment protection. The government launched a series of unemployment-related measures, including temporary job creation, mainly through public works, employment stabilization—for example, support for retaining employees and stabilizing small and medium-sized firms—vocational training and job placement, investment and start-up subsidies for venture enterprises, and extended income support for the unemployed.[128] The Employment Insurance Program had been adopted in 1993 and implemented in 1995. In quick succession—in four waves during 1998—coverage was extended from employees in large firms to all employees; eligibility criteria, such as a minimum contribution requirement, was relaxed; and the level of unemployment benefits was improved and their duration extended. For instance, the minimum daily amount of the job-seeking benefit, the main type of unemployment benefit, increased from 50 percent of the "minimum basic daily wage" to 70 percent in March 1998, and was to be increased again to 90 percent in January 2000.

Despite these efforts, however, the employment insurance remained too limited in scope to constitute an adequate protection against the now-rampant risk of unemployment and poverty. Neither the self-employed nor unpaid family workers were covered, nor before 2004 were workers employed for less than one month. There were also other restrictive qualifying criteria. The crisis pushed up the number of temporary and day workers. The old Livelihood Protection System was also totally inadequate in the face of soaring poverty. A program of conventional poor relief, it offered only minimal and discretionary support on very restrictive work ability and demographic criteria, and was subject to absolute budget constraints.

The second step was the introduction of a new form of social assistance, not as an extension of the old poor relief but as a completely new system in its place. The National Basic Livelihood Security Act of August 1999, implemented as of October 2000, broke with the old system both in philosophy and practice. Discretionary poor relief was replaced with rights-based social assistance, and the principle of minimal income support was abandoned. The underlying philosophy was the securing of a social minimum as a duty of the state. In the spirit of productive welfare, the principle of a guaranteed social minimum was combined with workfare measures to enhance employability and self-support ability. Able-bodied recipients were obliged to participate in self-reliance measures within the program in order to preserve their entitlement to support. Coverage was extended by abolishing the demographic test of the old system, and the level of support was raised according to a relative concept of poverty. The number of those eligible increased from 0.54 million people under the previous system in 1999 to 1.54 million people in 2000. Public expenditure on social assistance increased from 1.3 percent of the government budget in 1997 to 3.3 percent in 2001.[129] The government had taken on a new level of responsibility for the funding and provision of social welfare.

However, in spite of qualitatively new commitments, the Korean state remained a low spender on social welfare. Although the social security budget surpassed 10 percent of total central government spending in 2001, it was still at less than 2 percent of GDP in 2003. The productive welfare reform showed remarkable changes in the sense that the concepts of social right and social investment were introduced for the first time into the policy portfolio of the Korean state, but it is incorrect to interpret the extended welfare role of the state as a wholesale shift in the welfare regime. It is still predominantly a welfare state based on the politics of regulation.

CENTRAL DECISION MAKING AND LOCAL IMPLEMENTATION

The events of 1997 conspired toward a qualitative change in the Korean state. First, although it continued to govern with and through non-state actors and both the government–business and government–voluntarism coalitions persevered, the democratic state needed to co-opt assertive forces from below that the authoritarian state had been able to ignore or repress.

Second, the structure of the state itself changed. It continued to work in a centralized manner with the presidency retaining its position as the dominant institution, but both the National Assembly and local government became stronger players in public policy with increasing authority and autonomy. The government had to relinquish some of its powers of command.

Out of the first change, the democratization of decision making, came new policies, a secondary effect of which was to reinforce the second change. In social policy, the state made itself more of a provider state, but public provisions are perforce delivered locally. Implicit in central decisions on state provision was therefore a new role of policy implementation put on local government. This shifted the balance of power between central and local authorities and made central decision makers more than previously dependent on local implementing authorities with some measure of autonomy. There had not been much of a tradition in Korea for the central state having to elicit the compliance of local government agencies; that had been a given. By all accounts this came as a bit of a surprise to the Korean system. While the need to co-opt the relevant forces in decision making was readily understood, the need to co-opt local government actors in the interest of executing the will of the state was not in the same way recognized as a constraint on policy. Hence, the new Korean state met less difficulty in the reshaping of decision making than in the implementation of new decisions and new types of policies.

Decision Making

Kim Dae Jung won the presidential election on December 18, 1997, with 40.3 percent of the vote against 38.7 percent for the conservative ruling party's candidate and 19.2 percent for another conservative candidate. His hands were tied. The economy was in crisis. He had no majority mandate and no majority in the National Assembly. His tenure was constitutionally limited to one term. He was bound to fulfill the terms of the IMF agreement. And he was no less than his predecessor committed to economic reform under the banner of labor market flexibility.

His way out of that bind was the Tripartite Commission, which he was able to get established and working even before he had taken up his post as president and in spite of a conspicuous lack of enthusiasm on the part of everyone who would compose it. The unions were reluctant because they knew one inevitable outcome would be labor market flexibility, including reduced job security and more power for employers to lay off workers, which they would be corralled into legitimizing. Business was reluctant because they knew that institutionalized tripartism would cost them some of the advantage over labor they had been used to in the days of government–business bipartism. Top state officials were reluctant because they saw that emerging new state structures would undermine their power.

Nevertheless, the president-elect got his commission and got it to do for him what he wanted to smooth out the process of neo-liberal reform. After intensive but not protracted negotiations, including under temporal boycotts by labor representatives, the commission in February produced its historic "Social Pact for Overcoming the Economic Crisis" with more than 100 detailed proposals on a 10-point agenda.[130]

This pact covered not only labor issues but also other economic and political reforms, some of which had already been proposed by the president-elect's camp and required by the IMF. The gist of the pact was labor's approval of increasing labor market flexibility, especially the introduction of layoffs for "urgent managerial reasons," in return for the recognition of basic labor rights, the reform of corporate (*chaebŏl*) governance, and the enhancement of social security.

The Tripartite Commission was a new meeting ground between forces from above and from below in which they were able and allowed to slug out their differences. But it was more than that. Kim Dae Jung had a mixed agenda. He wanted to push through labor market reforms that had been too long in the making. Although not a radical but also not a Korean conservative, he was committed to a more balanced relationship between capital and labor and to a somewhat more progressive social agenda than his predecessors. He used the commission to manipulate both sides toward more cooperative relations and into accepting reforms they did not like.[131]

Under the influence of economic crisis, tripartism was initially effective, giving birth to the social pact in next to no time. But the implementation of the pact was not inevitable. Many in the labor movement thought they were paying too high a price for a place at the table and the opportunity to participate in national talks on public policy as equal partners. In February 1998, the Korean Confederation of Trade Unions held its national congress to ratify the social pact, but 184 delegates out of 272 voted against it. Since then, the KCTU was in and out of the Tripartite Commission and finally stayed out in 1999 in anger over the government's structural reforms.

Moreover, the Tripartite Commission faced structural weakness and was often crippled after the early period of crisis management. The transition from enterprise unionism to industrial unions and industry-wide bargaining was still underway. In a sense, social and labor policies were still subordinate to macroeconomic policy, since the Kim Dae Jung government was preoccupied with its primary goal of neo-liberal economic restructuring. State officials remained lukewarm, if not hostile. There were few devices underpinning the commission for implementation, monitoring, and evaluation of its agreements. The aim was to break down the traditional bipartite coalition between the state and major business groups, but old antagonisms persisted and new institutionalized cooperative relations among tripartite actors did not fully emerge.

There had long been pressure from below for a new system of social assistance. The People's Solidarity for Participatory Democracy had been established in 1994 as a "progressive citizens' movement" for social reform. This movement, although idealistic, was initially ineffective and poor in strategy and made little headway. The economic crisis, however, gave more resonance to its ideas. As of 1998, it was instrumental in forming a loose network of civil society organizations in favor of welfare reform. A petition was submitted to the National Assembly for a basic livelihood protection. Pressure was building from below by a combination of at least semi-organized power and a specific policy proposal.

The initial and instinctive response from above was negative.[132] The economy-related ministries, which were used to wielding veto power in public policy, were hostile and dismissive. The Ministry of Planning and Budget opposed the idea in the prevailing economic situation on the argument that extended social assistance would overburden public budgets and cause work-disincentive effects and welfare dependency.[133] The Ministry of Health and Welfare, as always relatively powerless and trapped in the old economy-first mindset, was unable to take up a new idea and give it forceful support. A draft bill lay dormant as neither governmental agencies nor political parties were actively pushing it. Although forces from below now had arenas to work in, the pressure they could mobilize was, democratization notwithstanding, on its own not enough.

The pro-welfare coalition now regrouped and in March 1999 formed a new movement under the title the Solidarity for Enacting the National Basic Livelihood Security Act. The pressure from below was kept up and intensified. This gave the president the opportunity he needed to appeal to the spirit of tripartism and against the opposition to social reform, which was essentially a vestige of the conservative past, and to establish the principle of a state-guaranteed social minimum as a fact on the ground. In a speech in Ulsan on June 21, 1999, he issued what became known as the "Ulsan Statement," that "a law for securing national basic living standards would be enacted so that the middle class and low-income families could enjoy decent living standards." Given the centralized, hierarchical order in the decision-making structure in Korea's strong presidential system, the Ulsan Statement gave a decisive impetus to the pressure that had built up from the pro-welfare alliance. In August 1999, the National Basic Livelihood Security Act was passed in the National Assembly. Tripartism was messy and far from impressive, but it had, at least for now, created a new vertical coalition that at this critical juncture was able to outmaneuver the old horizontal one.

Implementation

The decisions to improve and extend unemployment compensation and to institute a new and modern system of social assistance changed the character of state governance. As a regulator, the state had imposed the implementation of its will on non-state actors. As a provider, it imposed on itself a new duty and burden of implementation. It had not only to decide what should be done, but also itself to deliver the goods. That was to prove administratively difficult.[134]

Social support must logistically be delivered to recipients where they live, which is to say locally. For the provider state, the implementer is local government. The new character of state governance imposed massive new responsibilities on local agencies and local officials and thereby also shifted power downward in the state structure. The state that had depended on business and voluntarism for the execution of its will now made itself more than previously dependent on a network of local government workers dispersed throughout the territory, some under its own command and some under the command of local authorities. Unemployment benefits and active labor market programs under the employment insurance were handled at the local level by subsidiary organizations of the Ministry of Labor. The basic livelihood security was implemented through local governments both in terms of administration and, to some extent, finance.

Local government in Korea, as of the constitution of the Sixth Republic with considerable autonomy, is organized on three levels: provincial, district, and ward, the latter being a non-autonomous administrative unit. Provincial governments are essentially intermediaries, while it is mainly district governments that deliver services to residents, mainly through their underlying wards. The heads of provincial and district government are directly elected. Local autonomy is limited in that many local executive functions are delegated by the central government.

Local government is funded partly from local revenues and partly by transfers from the state. In 2000, the average local revenue contribution to provincial budgets was 59 percent, ranging from 95 percent in Seoul to 27 percent in the *Chŏlla* region.[135] Social assistance is funded differentially within a tied-grants system.[136] The budget for the National Basic Livelihood Security Act in Seoul is funded half by state subsidies and half from local revenue, the latter half being shared equally between the provincial government and district governments, who each provide a quarter of the total budget. For the other 15 provincial governments, 20 percent of expenditure is covered locally, and again shared equally between the provincial government and district governments, while the remaining 80 percent is covered by central government subsidies.

When the employment insurance was introduced in 1995, Regional Labor Offices under the Ministry of Labor, 46 in all, were charged with implementation. Their tasks were labor inspection, breaches of the Labor Standard Act, and the implementation of active labor market measures. With the expansion of the employment insurance coverage after the economic crisis of 1997, the government set up new Employment Security Centers for employment insurance services and separated these functions out from the Regional Labor Offices.

The post-1997 reforms had two broad aims: to lift income maintenance and to stimulate labor market integration and reintegration. The first aim was manifested in a recognized citizenship right to a social minimum. The second aim was to enhance employability and self-reliance by those able to work through a strategy of active labor market integration. The centrality of work and self-reliance was nothing new to the Korean welfare system, but prior to productive welfare these principles had not been supported by notable active labor market policies. For example, public spending on active labor market measures was estimated to only 0.1 percent of GDP as late as 1996.[137]

The way to see in detail how these aims were realized is to observe what was actually deliverable and delivered on the local level.[138] When we do, we see that the state was not able to move smoothly into the provider role. The Korean tradition was that the state got its will by getting others to deliver for it. This proved not straightforward in its new dependency on local government. It might have been unexpected that when the state in principle took control of delivery, it found it more difficult than it had been used to get its policies implemented. In the end, in the post-1997 reforms, less was delivered locally than decided centrally.

There were two reasons. First, there were decision deficits centrally, which became visible locally. Although the right to a social minimum was recognized in principle, restrictive entitlement conditions were retained in the systems that seriously limited their reach. For reasons rehearsed previously, only a minority of the unemployed (estimated to about 20 percent) were entitled to unemployment benefits.[139] Although improved, the level and duration of unemployment benefits were still less than generous by international standards.[140]

The basic livelihood security, which was the embodiment of the social minimum, in practice fell far short of that aspiration. The family support principle was retained in that eligibility for support continued to depend on the economic capacity of the household or extended family, and economic capacity to be defined more broadly than actual income. The household-based eligibility and means test caused many of the poor and needy to be excluded from support. With the incidence of poverty estimated at between 7 and 12 percent of the population, only about 3 percent were covered by the basic livelihood security.[141]

Secondly, there were implementation deficits locally. A first major difficulty was in the practical management of the family-support criteria, in particular in establishing whether extended family members were considered capable supporters. On the one hand, the circle of potential supporters was defined so broadly into the extended family that the task of establishing whether a potential recipient was in fact without relevant family support was extremely burdensome administratively. On the other hand, local administrative culture was such that officials tended to regard family support criteria favorably and as criteria they should seek diligently to uphold, to hold potential supporters to be duty-bound to take care of family members, and to keep pro-welfare activists who argued for a relaxation of family support criteria at arm's length. Likewise, in the employment insurance, local administrative culture would lean toward a restrictive interpretation of unemployment and the exclusion from support of those deemed voluntarily unemployed. Support would be more strictly limited locally than may have been intended centrally.

A second difficulty was in the management of the active labor market or workfare component of the new programs. Employment Security Centers were set up with the aim of providing an integrated "one-stop service" for employment insurance, training, re-training, job placement, and the like, but in large measure failed to provide the intended quality of service.

The basic livelihood security introduced a complicated conditional recipient system that was intended to operate by dividing recipients into two categories according to their employability or working ability. In practice, however, the categorization of recipients often did not reflect their work ability, in particular in that clients tended to be seen as employable in spite of an actual low level of work ability. Clients with work ability are supposed to be encouraged toward employment by engaging in self-reliance measures and training, but the implementation of this component of the social assistance typically strayed considerably from the intention of the policy. Often, local welfare officers were pessimistic about and disengaged from the workfare stimuli that were crucial to the policy design.

There were multiple reasons behind the implementation deficit locally, ranging from administrative capacity, via confusion in lines of authority and coordination, to an absence of local culture to engage proactively with new central government intentions. Local government capacity did increase—for example, the number of local welfare officers increased from 3,000 in 1998 to 9,000 in 2005.[142] But local agencies were still overwhelmed by heavy workloads and inadequate administrative and financial resources, and caseload-to-staff ratios remained well above the OECD norm.[143] Korea, for all its intended turn toward "productive welfare," remains at the bottom of the league among OECD countries in public expenditure on active labor market policies.[144]

When the government made itself more dependent on local implementers in the context of newly introduced local government autonomy, it experienced that "street-level bureaucrats" do not always share the goals, interests, and priorities of higher-ranking policy makers.[145] In many cases, the new policies met with active or passive local resistance. The perception of many local officials was of a gulf between central goals and local realities and of local realities not being appropriately reflected in policies made centrally by state elites without field-level experience.

Effective implementation of complex policies depends on coordination between and within various organizations, both between levels within government and between government and private-sector actors. Coordination can be conceptualized along three dimensions: the vertical (central–local), the horizontal at the central level, and the horizontal at the local level.[146] The implementation of both the extended employment insurance and the new basic livelihood security was lacking in coordination in all three dimensions. At the central level, the Ministry of Planning and Budget was as ever the super-ministry with veto power over spending that held back on the establishment of necessary administrative capacity for the new policies. While the Ministries of Health, Welfare, and Labor were in charge of policies, the Ministry of Government Administration and Home Affairs, with no substantial responsibility for policy, was in charge of personnel and administration, all of them engaged in competitions over turf. At the local level, there was limited experience in the management of large social programs, and welfare officers felt themselves to be working under administrative managers who had little expertise in social welfare.

The workfare component of the new policies was dependent on public–private sector coordination at the local level. But, in practice, joined-up governance at the periphery did not work well, and the consultative committees that were intended to generate public–private partnerships existed mostly in name only. The government also attempted to establish so-called local employment networks encompassing a variety of public and private actors by the devise of consultative bodies for the purpose and attached to the Employment Security Centers.[147] In reality, only a few centers operated consultative bodies in which the societal partners could participate.

Public policies can be conceptualized in terms of inputs and outcomes. Governments make decisions on inputs in order to generate intended outcomes. The converting of inputs into outcomes depends on decisions being implemented effectively and in accordance with intentions. Kim Dae Jung's social policy reforms are typically identified by inputs: new rules of unemployment compensation and social assistance. However, it turned out that the new responsibility for provision that the government accepted opened up an unexpected problem of implementation between inputs and outcomes. The reforms were more impressive in terms of inputs than outcomes, which fell short of what was intended because of a deficit of cooperative capacity between central and local government.

DEMOCRATIC MIXED GOVERNANCE

Until democratization, mixed governance, although often conflictual and messy, had in the end been made to work as an effective corporatist system. The government had been the decider, co-opting others into decision making in a controlled manner and just enough for them to allow themselves to be coerced and mobilized for the government's design. By the time of democratic consolidation, the old system was radically overturned. The government was no longer the autocratic decider. Non-state actors were no longer handmaidens. Labor had been brought into the fold and capital made less overpowering.

Democracy, predictably, saddled the government with new and extended responsibilities. Mixed governance persisted in the form of occupational welfare and voluntarism. The taking on of more of a provider responsibility opened up a new dimension of mixed governance, that of coordinated central and local government. In some ways, democratic mixed governance was to prove more of a challenge, at least initially, than had been the autocratic brand. It was more open, more legal, more legitimate, and more orderly, but also more complicated in that it had to operate through different levels of government with competing authorities. Korea was to learn painfully how hard it is to get normal mixed governance to work effectively. Central–local coordination is one of the most intractable difficulties in democratic governance, not least in social policy. The road from centrally decided inputs via implementation to real outcomes locally is simply terribly difficult. That difficulty hit the Korean state with full force in the aftermath of democratic consolidation. If 1961 had marked a first watershed transition for the Korean state to authoritarian exceptionalism, 1997 brought on a second radical transition, now to democratic normality. Korea had left the developmental state behind and reverted to normalized governance.

One consequence of normality, for the analyst, would be to temper the language of "the strong state." It is probably still correct to describe South Korea, comparatively, as a state-led society and a president-led state, but now with serious qualifications. State–society relations have become more balanced, and within the state the president is more *primus inter pares* and less of a commander.

Has orderly governance suffered? The ability of the center to impose its will is much reduced, but that is as it should be in a democratic system. The authoritarian state was effective but also seriously flawed in terms of corrupt practices, not to mention repression. The democratic state may look less impressive, as seen for example in its difficulties with the implementation of its own decisions, but was remarkably effective in the way it was able to steward forward much overdue reforms and to exploit the 1997 coincidence of democratic consolidation and economic crisis for that purpose. If democratic governance looks "messy," it may be worth remembering that the "mess" the authoritarian rulers tolerated to be able to impose their will was no less in quantity and more reprehensible in quality.

A second consequence of normality is a broadening of concern on the part of the government. The official Korea was long concerned with itself only and with its economic growth only. It is now, by both choice and necessity, taking on a wider agenda. One sign of this is on the family front. Korean families have been used to carrying the brunt of responsibility for the care of their members but are now crying out for help with the burden of caring. Korea's fertility rate is ultra-low, population ageing is progressing rapidly, and population numbers are turning from growth to decline. Family policy is becoming a new pillar of the welfare state and can be expected to be a strong government preoccupation in the years ahead.

A second front of new government activity is in international development cooperation. Korean people are coming to realize that their place in the sun as the 10th trading nation in the world comes with a responsibility of assisting poorer countries, contributing to peace in troubled areas, and preventing conflicts. In 2010 Korea became a full member of the Development Assistance Committee within the OECD. Development cooperation is so far a small area of activity for Korea, but its take-up marks a qualitatively important transition. A country that was recently itself poverty-stricken and dependent on aid from others is making itself an international donor country. This is another expected growth area for Korean governments and yet another sign of a once monomaniac state becoming a normal democratic state.

6

CONCLUSION: THE ANATOMY OF THE STATE

South Korea succeeded! The exclamation mark is in order. It was not inevitable; the other Korea failed. If we go back to around 1950, not much was expected of East Asia. The region was seen as underdeveloped, lacking in resources, and already overpopulated. Africa was then the arena of hope: vast in land and space, rich in resources, and with a new generation of forward-looking leaders.[148] The ultimate success is in the revenge of democracy. That success belongs to no government, and certainly to no authoritarian government, but to the nation and the endurance of its people.

ECONOMIC ADVANCEMENT

South Korea was under authoritarian rule for 26 years, with degrees of authoritarianism also before 1961 and after 1987. The analysis of this authoritarian state is not straightforward because it turns out to have been a state with two very different sides to it. In the use of force it was ruthless, and its history can be written as a story of an oppressive state. That is an accurate history—but still not a complete one. Our take on state analysis is to follow through from power to the use of power and from state structures to governance and outcomes. When we do that, and observe governance through the prism of social policy, we see governments working with more prudence than might be expected from a state under authoritarian and at times dictatorial control.

This represents a certain nuanced interpretation of Korean authoritarianism. We offer that interpretation against a backdrop of recognition that this was a period of harsh and in part uninhibited political repression. Nothing in our interpretation is intended to gloss over or excuse the ugliness of dictatorship. General Park and his friends took power illegally. They dissolved the National Assembly, put an end to civil liberties and freedom of the press, and banned political activity. One of their first initiatives, in 1961, was to create the Korean Central Intelligence Agency with far-reaching powers, including the power of arrest, and under the control of and reporting directly to the president. After 10 years, Park tightened the screws again and reined in the semblance of political normality that had evolved after 1963 in a coup within the coup and the introduction of the *Yushin* constitution. His means of political control included not only manipulations of elections and the constitution but also whole-scale purging of unreliable civil servants and officers; a massive use of secret police and spies throughout society; intimidation and arrest of political and union activists; trumped-up charges expedited by kangaroo courts; violent repression of demonstrations and threatening manifestations, at the cost of lives in unknown numbers; the shutting down of universities and newspapers; and censorship. All that is irrefutable fact and represents one side of the Janus-faced creation that was the strong state. It had another side to it, but the inclusion of the second face in the full description of this creature does not wipe out or change or modify or disguise the ugliness of the first face.[149]

Any serious government must deal with two imperatives: to hold power and to exercise governance. On one extreme are stable and orderly democratic governments. These hold power legitimately as long as they have voter support and need invest next to no effort in maintaining power as such. They are entirely governments of governance. At the other extreme are governments that hold power exclusively by force and that by choice or necessity more or less neglect governance and dedicate themselves fully to the preservation of power for its own sake or, for example, for the purpose of robbing national resources. One example would be the regime of Mobutu Sese Seko in Zaire from 1965 to 1997.

Between these extremes are systems in which governments, on the one hand, hold power with less than obvious legitimacy and, on the other, dedicate themselves at least to some degree to governance for the benefit of society and nation. Where legitimacy is weak, relatively more effort is usually invested in holding on to power, and governance is likely to suffer. Where there is stronger legitimacy, there is more scope for the government to move beyond power politics and into governance.

There is a delicate dialectic between legitimacy and governance. While legitimacy enables governance, also it is governance that makes or breaks legitimacy. A government that is seen to deliver for its people will gain legitimacy in their eyes. A prudent government that cannot take its power for granted would try to deliver governance in order to be seen as acceptable and thereby secure its grip on power by some measure of implicit acceptance in the population. It is therefore no mystery that authoritarian governments have often been activist in delivering welfare to their citizens, as was the case in the Soviet Union and its satellites in Eastern Europe.[150] It was in the interest of these governments to do good socially in order to prevent their populations from turning against them politically. When the autocrats in South Korea started very early to develop a welfare state there, this kind of purchase of legitimacy was very much what they were up to.

The authoritarian governments in South Korea were of a special kind among authoritarian governments. They were, on the one hand, pretty far out toward one extreme in the use of force to maintain power, but also, on the other hand, pretty far out toward the other extreme in delivering governance. They did use governance to buy legitimacy and to shore themselves up, but they were under constant pressure from below and could not trust legitimacy to be a sufficient basis of power, and were therefore reliant, when they saw it necessary, on the ruthless use of force.

This combination of being strong both in the use of force and in the delivery of governance is the specific feature of South Koran authoritarianism. That combination in turn grew out of two influences. First, a disillusionment with what was seen to be weak and disorderly government during the First and Second Republics. That enabled the generals to persuade themselves that South Korea was a difficult country to govern and one that needed the guidance of a very strong hand from above. They may well have been wrong in this. The Second Republic, although lasting no more than a year, had remade Korea democratic, and we cannot know what would have happened had democracy survived. Nor can we know what would have happened if, for example, Park had lost the election in 1971 to Kim Dae Jung, as he nearly did. Right or wrong, however, the generals were persuaded that Korea needed the kind of order and force they could impose.

Secondly, it was, paradoxically, with the coming of authoritarianism that the South Korean modernization project was articulated explicitly. The generals took power for the purpose of carrying the country forward toward the place in the sun that they saw for it.

The first of these influences justified in the eyes of the generals near inhibition in the use of force. The second influence pushed them toward activism in the delivery of governance. There was a connection. Governance was used to buy legitimacy and to temper the need for force, but the specific, perhaps unique, characteristic of South Korean authoritarianism is that it never became either strong in governance and therefore restrained in the use of force, or strong on force and therefore timid in governance. It was consistently strong in both dimensions, both negatively in repression and positively in governance. These were not primitive dictators. They were in all their reprehensibility also sophisticated in the sense of seeing themselves as, and being, agents of a project that was bigger than themselves. The view of those who took, held on to, and used power was that South Korea was to modernize come hell or high water, that there could not be modernization without strong governments, and that there could not be strong governments without force.

There is an uncanny similarity between South Korea during the years of autocracy and Germany in the first period of unification after 1871, at least for those of us who observe governance through social policy.[151] As Bismarck was in control in Germany, Park was in control in Korea. As Bismarck was at the head of a strong state, the Korean leader had the instruments of state power firmly in his hands. As Bismarck ruled with effectiveness, so also did Park. As Bismarck used power with reluctance in governance, preferring when possible to co-opt rather than to coerce, although doing so by showing himself ready to coerce when necessary, so also the Korean rulers. And as for Germany, social policy was a central instrument of rule, so it was in Korea. As Bismarck was able when necessary to govern against his own instincts and make concessions to opposing forces he despised and would rather have crushed, so also Park. He was perhaps not quite up there with Bismarck in sheer manipulative shrewdness, or in social policy innovativeness, but he was not far behind. In both cases, social policy was used to buy legitimacy, to pacify, and to manipulate, but also more broadly to help build the state and nation the rulers had in mind. The historian Norman Davies ascribes Bismarck's political genius to "a marvelous combination of strength and restraint," and for Isaiah Berlin he was "a great and an evil man."[152] Much of the same could be said for Park.

Park Chung Hee was a straight-laced military technocrat. He disliked the "mess" he saw others making of Korea, and he wanted to put things in order with the help of governments that knew how to get things done. His ideas of order were strength, hierarchy, and command. He disliked anything that could disturb that kind of order. He disliked business and businesspeople, who wallowed in corruption and could not be trusted to stay in line. One cannot imagine that he harbored any vision of a vibrant civil society in which voluntary agencies were the providers of essential services for the population. It is almost as if he, by inclination and setting aside communism, would have been more comfortable in North Korea than in the South.

Yet, when in power, he saw that "mess" was inevitable and that non-state actors could not just be put in their place in a chain of command. Only those who were weak and whom he did not need because they had no useful service to offer him, such as the trade unions, did he push down and away. Those who might have been able to stand up to him and whom he could make use of, he co-opted. He saw that they could be used, but also understood that he needed them. In the business community he encountered a pack of economic profiteers who had enriched themselves during the years of Rhee Syngman, and whom he despised and was minded to put away in jail and leave there. But instead, he entered into a, for him, unholy alliance with the *chaebŏl* and gave in to a particular brand of state-directed monopoly capitalism steeped in corruption that must have been distasteful to him. Instead of nationalizing the voluntary sector, and thereby ridding himself of a potentially threatening network of civil agencies involved in at least potential grassroots activism, he again struck a deal with the devil that allowed the voluntary sector to continue working and growing in return for delivering services he needed to have delivered to the population but that it was not in the economic or administrative capacity of his governments to deliver themselves. There is a strong state here, but one that understands the art of co-opting as well as of commanding.

The state–business alliance in Korea is well known. Less well known has been the parallel alliance of state and voluntary sector, parallel also in coming into shape as early as or earlier than the state–business alliance. This alliance sits oddly with the idea that in Korea, public policy flowed directly from the strong state. The Korean welfare state was made by the presidency. That was the case with all public policy in the authoritarian period, and has not changed all that much since. But the *management* of the welfare state was in the hands of a broad coalition of state, business, and voluntarism. When we observe these structures together, we see a very particular kind of strong state. It calls the shots and instructs its partners about what is expected of them. But it also works *with* partners. What we see is not a state doing the job, but one co-opting others to get the job done for it in some kind of togetherness in which there is give and take on both sides.

The Korean rulers, certainly President Park, dealt with their own apparatus of government in much the same way as they dealt with society. They set themselves up to be in charge, in control, and in command. They hired people they trusted, purged those they disliked, promoted those who were faithful, and spied on those who were suspect. But then, on this understanding of who was in charge, they turned to flattery. They bought loyalty with privileged pensions. They pulled officials into the orbit of power and listened to them and consulted with them. They created institutions for their participation. They engaged advisors and experts whom they did not patronize but allowed platforms of independence and influence. The skill that stands out here, as vis-à-vis society at large, is the skill of co-optation.

In governance, even the authoritarian governments were strong in an indirect way, less in doing than in getting others to do as they wanted. Again, the contrast with the second reincarnation of the Korean nation in the North could not be sharper. They started from the same base, but in the North a strong state determined to not only manage but to run in detail its society brought its population to serfdom, ignorance, and famine.[153] In the South, the recipe for success was mixed governance.

There is a lesson here for any state that will be strong. Strength notwithstanding, the state is not likely to be able to shape events creatively in its country if it puts its trust (in Joseph Nye's terminology again) in hard power only.[154] That's the story of failure in North Korea. It is simply impossible for any state to *order* its society to be efficient. It may get obedience but is unlikely to get effort. If it wants not just control but also development, like it or not there is no other way than to mobilize others by way of restraint and soft power. The cardinal feature of the polity, writes S. E. Finer in *The History of Government*, is what he calls "the problem of baron management." The king can "... only give effect to his orders through them [the barons]. Therefore they must be induced to give enthusiastic support (the best outcome) or acceptance (the next best) and discouraged from foot-dragging or, at the very worst, open resistance."[155] It is much the same for a modern state in a modern society. Effectiveness of rule does not spring from the strength of the state but from its ability to get officials and citizens to comply with its wishes, at least with acceptance and preferably with some active participation. Any leader who tries to obtain that with hard power will fail, and only those who have some gift for the use of soft power can succeed.[156]

Even the South Korean state, which during the main build-up of modernization was centralized, hierarchical, powerful, and ruthless, was in governance essentially at the mercy of others on whom it had to rely in order to impose its will. It certainly had the means of coercion at its disposal, and the will and ability to use such means, but those means and that strategy were of use to it mainly for protecting itself and maintaining what it saw to be necessary order. The forcing of others to efficiency with the help of raw coercion is not available to any state. Only rulers who are able to understand this and to rule accordingly, however strong they be, have the potential to be effective. The Korean authoritarian governments, unusually among autocracies, seem to have had or stumbled upon a keen awareness of this complexity of governance and were able to govern with much care and a good deal of restraint in spite of a total absence of fear in the use of force.

It's one thing for a state to be strong, and something else for it to be both strong and effective. A state in which strong levers of power are centralized and that power available to be unleashed on the decision of a small elite is a strong state. But strength makes no state effective. That comes to a strong state only if it is able to use its power smartly. The Korean strong state embodied these qualities: the ability to let its population taste the harsh reality of state power when necessary but also the ability to restrain itself and to work with rather than against non-state actors. No one would pretend, to put it carefully, that politics in Korea during the authoritarian period were a pretty sight. But even so, these governments were not *just* repressive. They were effective with an effectiveness that did not flow directly from the state, but was generated through social coalitions. Those coalitions, in particular with business, were complex and in part ugly, but in the end made to operate productively. To buy effectiveness, even a strong state has to pay something. It has to recognize that it is itself dependent on others who may not have the power to oppose it, but who always have the power to not work with it. The Czech dissident and later president Vaclav Havel called it "the power of the powerless."[157] A strong state that is ambitious for its society and not merely for itself cannot do as it wants or as its strength would permit. By having to co-opt others, it needs to some degree to let itself be co-opted by them. It must accommodate itself to the will of those on whom it depends for translating the power that sits in the state into development in society.

What is infuriating for the observer and difficult for the analyst is that South Korean authoritarianism was successful not only for itself but also for its nation. It was in fact least successful for itself. The authoritarian period came to an end against the will of the autocrats. In 1987, the regime gave in to democratic elections in spite of a very deliberate effort to continue the authoritarian line. But it was successful in its project. It engineered economic growth and laid the foundations for continued economic growth. It was even arguably over-successful in that it in spite of itself produced the inevitability of its own demise. South Korea was a democratic country in which democratic government was interrupted by a period of autocratic rule. That autocracy, however, did not come about in order to interrupt the national project that had started to emerge under more or less democratic guidance, but to improve on it. In this respect there was a clear line of continuity from democracy through authoritarianism and to democracy again. The modernization project was not of any single government's making, authoritarian or not, but was the great constant in South Korean political life in the second half of the 20th century. Park articulated the project and put it to use for his own good, but it was still a project he had inherited and was bound to continue. When events then again moved in favor of democracy, it was in the end not in the power of even the powerful Korean autocrats to prevent their own downfall, because that would have required a level of repression that would also have crushed the modernization that was the purpose, rationale, and excuse of their very existence. Governments dedicated to force can and are likely to repress as long as they are able to and irrespective of costs, but governments that have bound themselves to a project of betterment for their nation just cannot do that endlessly.

It is difficult to find an appropriate label to describe South Korean authoritarianism. It represents a fairly unique kind of government, ruthlessly repressive but also progressively successful. It is not enough to describe these governments as repressive, as that would put them in the same category with the many deplorable governments of the world that have been only repressive. Nor would it seem appropriate to describe autocracy in Korea as, for example, enlightened autocracy. That label is generally used for governments that hold the power to be repressive but use that power with a very light hand, which was not the case in Korea.

The conventional interpretation of the Korean state is "strong." But that does not capture the delicate balance between force and restraint that was the essential characteristic of Korean authoritarianism. There was force but also direction, there was repression but also mission, and there was brutality but also that undercurrent of project and modernization. These governments used their strength to be able to rule, but then governed with the help of restrained strength. This is the balance that becomes visible in the meeting ground of our state analysis and social policy narrative—by following through to observing carefully not just how the state was constituted but also what it *did*, and by undertaking that observation through the analysis of social policy governance. This is the combined analysis that enables us to see that the authoritarian Korean state was a strong state, but that strength was still not its defining characteristic. The identity of this state is to be found not in power but in the *use* of power, in its ability to govern rationally so as to make things—astonishing things—happen in and to Korean society.

Our analysis neither adds to nor subtracts from what is well enough known about the use of government force. Nor is it in any way our intention to suggest that governance excuses force. But we think we add something to the understanding of the Korean state and that we do so through a deeper analysis than a pure power analysis. Korean modernization grew out of state practices that differed sharply in their two manifestations. While in dispensing force it was self-sufficient and reliant only on the apparatus of state under its own command, in dispensing governance it was dependent on non-state actors. In the exercise of force it could *command* obedience, but in governance it had to *ask for* compliance.

South Korea took off to modernization through the leadership of a strong state. Was it thanks to authoritarianism that it was able to modernize? We cannot know if Korea would have succeeded under a different system of rule, but we can say that when it did succeed under authoritarian rule, it was *not* because the regime was authoritarian. It was because the authoritarian regime governed in the way it did and because its way was an unusual way for autocratic regimes— we have called it *mixed governance*. It was thanks to the regime being less authoritarian in governance than it could have been and had the power to be. This was not your run-of-the-mill tin-pan dictatorship. It was a regime of shrewdness and sophistication. Without that extraordinary shrewdness, authoritarianism in Korea would, as has authoritarianism mostly, have brought the country down and not built it up.

THE WELFARE STATE

The American Military Government brought with it voluntarism, which would become the first pillar of the Korean welfare state. The military coup launched statutory social insurance and promoted occupational welfare as the second pillar. In the drama of democratic consolidation and economic crisis, the state stepped out of its self-imposed reserve as a regulator and took on, in addition, more of a role of welfare provider, making state provision the third pillar of a now relatively advanced welfare state. What was first the arch-typical *developmental* welfare state matured step by step into, simply, a welfare state that does not need any qualifying adjective to explain it. It is still not a conspicuously generous welfare state in the level of provisions, but it has evolved from being strategically selective to becoming socially inclusive.

Korea was modernizing. The building of a welfare state was a part of that project. From a base in meager poor relief, the state became more socially responsive and the welfare state more inclusive. Economically advanced countries are perforce welfare states, all the more so if they are democracies. They organize social policies in different ways, but it does not work in the modern world to just let social problems lie where they fall. In Korea, it was obvious and necessary that social protection would be gradually broadened and improved.

But at the same time that the Korean welfare state was an outcome of modernization, a dependent variable in our analysis, it was also an instrument of modernization—an independent variable. It was used by rulers who were determined to lift Korea out of humiliation and backwardness as one of their levers. That, too, was logical. State-regulated or provided welfare has served autocratic and democratic regimes alike as a tool of rule. Korea is an exemplary case. Authoritarian rulers started it, and where they left off democratic governments continued. The dictators were nothing if not competent. From day one, General Park turned to the social policy of legitimization as instinctively as to the improvement of state espionage. For the authoritarian innovators in social reform, the welfare state they started to build was an instrument of order, control, and mobilization. It was for the good of the people but also, and for that very reason, helpful for those who ruled over them.

With democracy, the state acquired normal legitimacy and did not in the same way need the political instrumentality of social policy. It did not need social policy less, however—rather the contrary—but for different reasons. The welfare state that had been established as an instrument of rule now became more normally *only* an instrument of social protection.

DEMOCRACY

The welfare state was launched as an instrument of mobilization for a regime that proved itself remarkably shrewd in the art of governing. It was not least in its ability to mobilize society that this state displayed its competence. It mobilized its own servants. It mobilized experts. It mobilized rural populations and industrial workers and their families to self-betterment in the cultural revolution of the *Saemaul* Movement. It to some degree mobilized trade unions, at least by not wiping them out. It used the developmental welfare state to mobilize business. It turned foreign voluntarism into a national capacity and mobilized it for the management of social services.

Mobilization is a strategy with consequences. Those who are mobilized survive, live, and sometimes prosper. Many authoritarian regimes have preferred to crush society; in South Korea, in contrast, society was mobilized. The price of mobilization, from the point of view of the rulers, is to allow others influence. The officials and experts who were mobilized used their influence to fortify the modernization project. They saw themselves to be apolitical, but they were men of the world and brought an ethos of worldly sophistication to the partnership with their masters. They looked to the advanced countries of the world and saw, for example, that there would be no modern Korea without a welfare state. The rural people and factory workers who were mobilized in countless *Saemaul* projects were thereby given a voice so that the government that had given them that voice could not then turn around at will and just ignore what they said. Trade unions had a hard time of it, but they did survive with some measure of autonomy. Businesses and voluntary agencies became indispensible partners in governance.

By the strategy of mobilization, the authoritarian rulers not only led Korea to economic development but also built it up as a society rich in institutions. In the civil service, a centuries-old meritocratic tradition of bureaucratic rationality survived to some degree. Institutional meeting grounds were created in which masters and servants collaborated and civil servants were given importance. The role of expert advisor was made prominent and, again, institutions were created for serious and durable deliberations over public policy. The *Saemaul* Movement created quasi-government institutions of all kinds across the country. Tripartism was a tested technique in industrial relations long before Kim Dae Jung made a success of it in driving through labor market flexibility in the aftermath of economic crisis. And, as ever, businesses and voluntary agencies prospered.

The strong state-dominated society but also, paradoxically perhaps and probably not by design, filled it with life. The society it bequeathed to democracy was not one of monolithic and dictatorial social structures, but a pluralistic one of varied and vibrant institutions. How fundamentally different this was from the legacy of authoritarianism in Russia and Eastern Europe! There, autonomous institutions had been crushed, and when the old regimes were swept away there was nothing for the new ones to work with. They had to start from scratch and build up institutions again, from business via civil society to public administration. That process has been chaotic and difficult and has, after more than 20 years, still long to run for a new normality to be found. In Korea, there was no similar difficulty. Authoritarianism was pushed aside, the constitution was quickly redrafted, and democratic rule took over. The institutions of a reasonably pluralistic social and political order were there, alive and well, and democracy could without further serious drama find its footing in a gradual process of transition until consolidated 10 years after the breakthrough.

THE SOCIAL ORIGINS OF SUCCESS

In the first half of the 20th century, Korea was humiliated by colonialism and destroyed by war and division. It had to start afresh. It did that by adopting a project that grew out of its history: the resurrection of a nation that could stand proud in the world. This project—or vision—was of paramount importance as a source of inspiration and direction. It transcended all disagreement, conflict, and strife in the second part of the century. It represented the will of the nation to seriously make something of itself. But the will to improve is only half the story; there must also be ability.

In South Korea, the project was established and survived as one of modernization. That was not inevitable. In the North, it perverted to nostalgia, although there it had also started as modernization, at first more successfully than in the South in terms of economic growth. Why did South Korea stay the course?

South Korea was established as a democratic state. In part, a democratic constitution was imposed by the United States, but underlying was a pressure for democracy by forces from below, which was thereby given authority and which was subsequently never defeated. That pressure made itself felt both at dramatic junctures—first at the moment of independence in 1945 and then again in the April Revolution in 1960, at the fall of the Fourth Republic in 1980, and in the June Uprising in 1987—and continuously as constant pinpricks of demonstrations, manifestations, worker and student unrest, and the like.

One reason why the demand for democracy eventually prevailed was that South Korea first succeeded economically. With the advance of capitalist affluence, the case for authoritarian necessity could eventually no longer be sustained. Since the argument had been that autocracy was a necessary evil for the greater purpose of economic growth, it could not be maintained as necessary once economic growth had been delivered. Indeed, when forces from below gelled into taking on a weakened authoritarian elite in 1987, it was unable to withstand the pressure. In the long run, with economic advancement and South Korea in the Western world camp, the demand for democracy could not be kept down. Re-democratization should in hindsight probably be seen as inevitable.

Very early, South Korea undertook land reform. The importance of early and radical land reform for subsequent progressive developments can hardly be overstated.[158] The consequences were three. First, it was a boost to the young state that proved itself capable of controversial decision making and complicated administration. Second, it transformed the class structure, eliminating the old elite of large landowners and the influence of its obvious conservatism and cleared the ground for a new class of entrepreneurial capitalists. And third, it increased agricultural productivity and pushed a whole generation of young rural people into education and from there into productive industrial labor.

South Korean society was unruly. Shifting governments constantly faced trouble, dissent, protests, demonstrations, and at times revolts from various forces from below. But at the same time, and somewhat contrary to appearance, the Korean people, immersed in a Confucian culture of respect, did let themselves be led and mobilized by those in authority. Shifting governments made full use of this propensity for compliance. It turned to mass mobilization in the *Saemaul* Movement and pulled both rural and industrial constituencies through a cultural revolution. Remarkably, and outrageously, one is tempted to say, even that succeeded.

Authoritarian rule, although brutal, turned out to be progressive for South Korea. This was because it brought will and ability to the project to which it bound itself—but also because of the coincidence that it was itself literally shot down before it could run its course when President Park was killed. What would have happened had President Park been able to continue is obviously not known, but most authoritarian regimes, if allowed to, sooner or later pervert into authoritarianism for their own sake, and the signs were there for that to have happened in South Korea as well.

In much of the second half of the 20th century, across the world authoritarian government was more the rule than the exception. The general experience of 20th-century authoritarianism is one of ineffective rule. It was long a strongly prescribed theory that there was a trade-off between democracy and authoritarianism: democracy was superior in representativeness and fairness but authoritarianism in effective rule—for example, for economic development. In fact, however, democracy, generally if not always, has proved superior to autocracy in effectiveness as well as fairness.[159] Autocracy in Latin America was a crude form of neo-feudalism that stood in the way of development and was swept aside toward the end of the century. Autocracy in Africa has often been little more than kleptocracy with scant concern at all for populations. In Europe, autocracy collapsed, first in Portugal, Spain, and Greece and then in the Soviet Union and Eastern Europe, in part under the weight of economic failure. Asia was long predominantly authoritarian, with the notable exceptions of India and Japan, and here, unusually, with examples of effective authoritarianism, of which South Korea, and perhaps Taiwan, is the prime example.

The pure form of modern autocracy evolved, at least in principle, in the Soviet bloc. This was totalitarian autocracy with the state as an all-powerful and awesome force. Society was absorbed in the state so that there were no competing institutions of autonomy. There were individuals and families and there was the state, but nothing between: no autonomous businesses, no unions, no associations, no free institutions of civil society, no free press—nothing. This form of authoritarianism was long seen to be sophisticated and effective. For example, in the notorious "kitchen debate" between then American Vice President Richard Nixon and Soviet Premier Nikita Khrushchev at the American National Exhibition in Moscow in 1959, Khrushchev no doubt believed that the Soviet economy would overtake the American one, and Nixon probably feared that might happen. Indeed, the theory of autocratic effectiveness remained credible until the fall of the Berlin Wall in 1989.

The South Korean experience could be seen as a vindication of this theory, but that interpretation would be entirely false. Authoritarian government there was radically different from the ideal model and never resulted in the imbalanced state–society relationship of the pure model. It was harsh in the way it took and held on to power, and on this side of the equation it generally eliminated competing institutions. But it did not at all conform to the ideal model in the way it dispensed governance. Here, far from eliminating non-state institutions, it vitalized such institutions and gave them roles and functions in its project. If civil society is made up of those institutions that live and operate in the space between individuals and the state, then authoritarianism in Korea was of a kind that worked with and stimulated such institutions and let civil society thrive.

We started this book with two questions: How could a destroyed country in next to no time become a sophisticated and affluent economy? And how could a ruthlessly authoritarian regime metamorphose with relative ease into a stable democratic polity? The answers to these questions are found, finally, in two levels of analysis. First, economic modernization was state led through a combined use of hard and soft power. The use of hard power, while considerable and conspicuous, explains little or nothing. It was the more unlikely reliance on relative soft power that enabled society to be mobilized and led. It was by mobilization more than by command that the state provided leadership, economically and otherwise.

Second, political modernization eventually became inevitable because of a constant underlying pressure for democracy that weakened autocratic leaders could not in the long run contain with force. The reason democracy could then persist and consolidate was both that an apparatus of effective governance was in place in the state system that new democratic rulers could take over and work with, and that the mode of governance that had long been pursued had, inadvertently or not, propped up non-state institutions so that a social structure was in place that could engage with the reformed state to create a normal, balanced state–society relationship.

NOTES

CHAPTER 1

1 See Amsden 1989, Wade 1990, Haggard 1990, Evans 1995, Cho and Kim 1998, Woo-Cumings 1999, Kohli 2004, Cumings 2005.

2 But see Im 2009.

3 See Gough 2001.

4 A *chaebŏl* is a large capitalist organization, usually based on a single family having controlling interests in a variety of companies, similar to the *Zaibatsu*.

5 But see Clifford 1994, Kim 2004, and Nam 2009.

6 The hard and soft power logic is from Nye 2008.

7 Some of the atrocities of the Korean War are now being documented by the South Korean Truth and Reconciliation Commission, which was set up in 2005 under a mandate from the National Assembly.

8 The label "revolution" is attached to these events by Cumings 2005. What is revolution or not in South Korean history is not easy to say. The events of 1960 brought down a dying regime but did not establish a durable alternative. The Second Republic was brought down by yet another revolution in 1961, which ushered in 26 years of authoritarianism. Authoritarianism was first seriously challenged in the *Kwangju Rebellion* in 1980 and eventually brought to an end with the help of a powerful mass action from below in 1987, events that are commonly referred to more modestly as the *June Uprising*. This brought democracy back in, although in a gradual process without a trace of revolutionary flair attached to it.

9   Cho 2003
10 Park 1963, Chun 2006
11 Lee 1997
12 On the dictatorial character of authoritarianism, see Lee 2006 and Im 1987.
13 On the Chun government, see Haggard and Moon 1990.
14 See Diamond and Kim 2000.
15 Kim D. J. 1987, 1999, 2000

CHAPTER 2

16 Lee 1968, Kwon 1997
17 Cumings 2005, pp. 149–150
18 Woo 1991
19 Park 1963, p. 177
20 The Swedish connection is perhaps not generally known—for example, it is not prominently mentioned in articles and obituaries following Kim's death in 2009. However, according to Kim himself in a conversation in 1997 with Professor Joachim Palme, the son of the late Olof Palme, Swedish prime minister at the time of the kidnapping, Kim felt himself to be in debt for his life to Olof Palme for using his American contacts to push for American authorities to intervene.
21 Kang et al. 2008
22 Son 1981
23 Choe 1991
24 Oh 1975
25 Im 1987
26 Whang 1981
27 Oh 2002
28 There is now a considerable literature on the (East Asian) developmental welfare state, including Jones 1990; Oniz 1991; Deyo 1992; Adelman 1997; Ku 1997; Goodman et al. 1998; Woo-Cumings 1999; Holliday 2000; Tang 2000; Hort 2000; Jacobs 2000; Ramesh 2000, 2003; Gough 2001, 2004; Adam et al. 2002; Holliday and Wilding 2003; Mkandawire 2004; Mishra et al. 2004; Wong 2004; Kwon 2005; Walker and Wong 2005; Doner et al. 2005; Estevez-Abe 2008; and Haggard and Kaufman 2008.
29 Kwon 2005
30 On the Korean welfare state, see Kwon 1999, 2004; Joo 1999; Lee 1999; Kim 2002; Shin 2003; Woo 2004; Peng 2004; Mishra et al. 2004; Hong and Song 2006; Hwang 2006; Yi 2007; Kim 2007; Lee 2008; Alcock and Craig 2009; and Chung 2009.
31 As documented by Yunjeong Yang in her DPhil dissertation, *Work in Later Life*, University of Oxford, 2010.
32 Kwon 1998
33 On power hard, soft, and smart, see Nye 2008.

CHAPTER 3

34   Cumings 2005, pp. 335, 340–341
35   Reeve 1963, p. 6
36   Satterwhite 1994
37   Oh 1968, p. 83
38   Park 1991
39   Kim, J.-R. 1995, pp. 262–266, 433–437
40   Stern et al. 1995
41   Office of Labor Affairs 1980
42   Haggard and Collins 1994, pp. 59–64
43   Kim and Yoo 2000, p. 154
44   Yang et al. 1990, p.16
45   Park 1970, pp. 58–59
46   Kim, I. 1998
47   Kang et al. 1991, pp. 90–109
48   Federation of Korean Trade Unions 1979, pp. 620–621
49   Woo 1991
50   Kim, H. K. 1997, p. 163
51   Council of Economic Organizations 1991
52   Kwon and O'Donnell 2001, p. 163
53   Lee, K. K. 1998
54   Lee 2005
55   Federation of Korean Trade Unions 1979, pp. 266, 278, 283
56   Han 1974, pp. 187–197
57   Federation of Korean Trade Unions 1979, pp. 569–577
58   Federation of Korean Trade Unions 1979, p. 607
59   Federation of Korean Trade Unions 1979, pp. 621–623, 651
60   Korea Employers Federation 1990, p. 117
61   Choi et al. 2001, pp. 214–215
62   Im 1997
63   Yi and Lee 2005
64   Yi 2007, pp. 127, 129
65   Korea Employers Federation 1990
66   Yi 2007
67   Yi 2007
68   Lee and Yoo 2009

CHAPTER 4

69   Gough 2001, p. 174
70   Kuhnle and Selle 1992; Johnson 1999
71   The default definition of the Johns Hopkins Center consists of the five cri-
      teria: first, voluntary organizations must hold some form of organizational

and institutional structure (formality); second, they must have a certain degree of institutional separation from the government (constitutional independence); third, surpluses cannot necessarily be ruled out, but the maximization of profits is not the primary purpose of the organization (nonprofit-distributing); fourth, they decide their own constitutions, administrative structures, policies, and activities (self-governing); and fifth, some meaningful degree of voluntary participation should be included in the actual conduct of the agency's activities (voluntarism). For more details, see Salamon and Anheier 1997.

72 Park et al. 2004

73 As per 1997, cf. Park et al. 2004.

74 Korean Association of Voluntary Agencies 1995, pp. 67–69

75 Lee, H. K. 1998

76 Ch'oe 1996

77 Editorial Committee for the History of Korean Military Revolution 1963

78 Yi 2003, Wolch 1990

79 The term "coercive isomorphism" is from DiMaggio and Powell 1991; also, refer to Meyer and Rown 1977.

80 Federation of Korean Industries 1998, Hwang 1998

81 Editorial Committee for the History of Korean Military Revolution 1963, p. 1303

82 Kim, T. 2008, p. 832

83 Lim and Kong 2001, Piven and Cloward 1979

84 Ministry of Health and Social Affairs 1992, pp. 9–10

85 Presidential Committee on the Globalization Campaign 1998, p. 344

86 Lee and Rhee 1999, Haggard 2000

87 Hahn and McCabe 2006

88 For more details on micro-productive and macro-distributive, refer to Deakin 2001.

89 Yi 2005, pp. 58–59

90 Community Chest of Korea 2002

91 On corporatism, see Taylor 1995, Wiarda 1997, McNamara 1999, Streeck 2006.

92 Office of the President 1978, p. 374

93 Chun 1984, pp. 8, 26

94 Roh 1990, p. 191

95 Kim, Y. S. 1995, p. 272

96 Presidential Committee on the Globalization Campaign 1995, pp. 158–160

97 Kim 1999; Office of the President 1999

98 Giddens 1998

99 Lewis 1990, Salamon 1995

100 Editorial Committee for the History of Korean Military Revolution 1963, pp. 1291–1292
101 National Association for Disaster Relief 1987, p. 210
102 Piven and Cloward 1971, Cawson 1982
103 Ministry of Health and Social Affairs 1985, pp. 265–271
104 Presidential Committee on the Globalization Campaign 1998, p.175
105 Kim, Y. 2008
106 Mishra et al. 2004
107 Ministry of Home Affairs 1980
108 Durkheim 1997, pp. 310–322
109 Kuhnle and Selle 1992, p. 30
110 Hahn and McCabe 2006, Kim 2007
111 Ministry of Government Administration and Home Affairs 2002, p. 192
112 Dahrendorf 2001
113 See Allen and Thomas 2000, Mayhew 2005, Deacon 2007.

CHAPTER 5

114 For all these tripartite bodies including the Minimum Wage Council, the Industrial Relations Reform Commission, and the Tripartite Commission in more detail, see Korea Labor Institute 1999.
115 Chung 2001, p. 18
116 Kwon 1999, Oh 1999, Shin 2003
117 In the 2004 elections, the progressive Democratic Labor Party, based on the KCTU, emerged as the third-largest Assembly bloc. The entrance of the Democratic Labor Party as the non-regional progressive party into the parliament can be attributed partly to the newly introduced "two-vote scheme" within the existing single-member district system. The new electoral scheme gives voters two ballots, one for the preferred candidate in their constituency and another for their favored party. The second vote determines the number of parliamentary members each party is assigned in terms of the partial scheme of proportional representation under the first-past-the-post system.
118 Oh 1999, p. 197
119 OECD 2000, p. 47
120 Kim, H.-R. 2000, p. 60
121 See Kim, S. 2000, pp. 106–108. The citizens' movement groups in Korea also differ from the "new social movements" in advanced industrial societies. In Western Europe, the new social movements emerged as an alternative to the "conservative" labour movements; raised new issues like peace, environmental safety, and gender equality; tried to transcend materialism and the left–right distinction; and relied on radical movement strategies. While the citizens' movements in Korea are similar to those movements in addressing various post-industrial issues, the

Korean movements' goals are still materialistic, such as economic justice and equality, and their strategies are moderate and reformist.

122 Kingdon 1984, p. 151
123 IMF 1997
124 See Wade and Veneroso 1998.
125 Cumings 2005, p. 331
126 Presidential Committee for Quality of Life 1999
127 Presidential Commission on Policy Planning 1999
128 Ministry of Labor 2001
129 *Health and Welfare Statistical Yearbook* 2001, 2002
130 For the detailed issues, see Korea Labor Institute 1999.
131 In his book, *Mass-Participatory Economy* (1996), Kim Dae Jung emphasised "the freedom of legitimate labour movements," "cooperative labour-management relations," and the end of "special favour for the *chaebŏl*."
132 See Ahn 2000.
133 Ministry of Planning and Budget 1999
134 For a more detailed discussion of theoretical and methodological issues for implementation—i.e., the analytical framework, research methods for empirical studies, rationale for local case study sites, and interview schedules—and the rich detail of empirical findings, see Lee 2008, 2009.
135 Ministry of Government Administration and Home Affairs 2000
136 To reduce financial disparities among local governments and induce balanced development between them, the central government provides subsidies to local governments through a system of tied grants (referred to in Korea as a "matching fund system"). Under this financing mechanism, a poorer local government often gets more funds than a relatively well-off local authority for financing otherwise similar projects. In principle, the contribution of the central government through state subsidies is conditioned on the participation of other tiers of local government.
137 Martin 1998
138 See also recent implementation studies such as Hill and Hupe 2002, O'Toole 2000, Barrett 2004.
139 Korea Institute for Health and Social Affairs 2005
140 Hwang 2005, p. 34; OECD 2000 p. 85
141 Ministry of Health and Welfare 2001b, p. 14; Chung and Choi 2003, p. 59
142 *Health and Welfare Statistical Yearbook* 2006
143 OECD 2000
144 See Keum 2005, pp. 151–152.
145 Lipsky 1980
146 Exworthy and Powell 2004
147 See Ministry of Labor 2005.

CONCLUSION

148   On the bright future of Africa, see Gunther 1955.

149   See Lee 2006.

150   See Rimlinger 1971.

151   See Mommsen 1981.

152   Davies 1997, p. 841

153   On what has become of daily life in North Korea, see Demick 2010.

154   Nye 2008

155   Finer 1997, pp. 295–296

156   See Ringen 2008, 2009.

157   Havel 1985, originally in Czech in 1978.

158   On the importance of land reform for transition to democracy or not, see Moore 1966.

159   Dahl 1998

REFERENCES

Adam, E., M. V. Hauff, and M. John, eds. *Social Protection in Southeast and East Asia.* Singapore: Friedrich Ebert Stiftung, 2002. Print.

Adelman, I. "Social Development in Korea, 1953–1993." *The Korean Economy 1945–1995.* Eds. D. Cha, K. Kim, D. Perkins. Seoul: Korean Development Institute, 1997. Print.

Ahn, B. Y. "Analysis of Enactment Procedures of National Basic Livelihood Security Act." *Korean Journal of Public Administration* 38(1) (2000): 1–50. Print.

Alcock, P., and G. Craig, eds. *International Social Policy: Welfare Regimes in the Developed World.* Basingstoke: Palgrave Macmillan, 2009. Print.

Allen, T. and A. Thomas, eds. *Poverty and Development into the 21st Century.* Oxford: Oxford University Press, 2000. Print.

Amsden, A. H. *Asia's Next Giant: South Korea and Late Industrialization.* New York: Oxford University Press, 1989. Print.

Appelbaum, R. P., and J. Henderson, eds. *States and Development in the Asian Pacific Rim.* Newbury Park: Sage Publications, 1992. Print.

Barrett, S. M. "Implementation Studies: Time for a Revival? Personal Reflections on 20 Years of Implementation Studies." *Public Administration* 82(2) (2004): 249–62. Print.

Cawson, A. *Corporatism and Welfare: Social Policy and State Intervention in Britain.* London: Heinemann, 1982. Print.

Cho, H. Y., and E. Kim. "State Autonomy and Its Social Condition for Economic Development in South Korea and Taiwan." *The Four Asian Tigers: Economic*

Development and the Global Political Economy. Ed. E. Kim. San Diego: Academic Press, 1998. Print.

Cho, S. G. "Land Reform and Capitalism in Korea." *The History of the Korean Capitalist Development Model and its Crisis*. Ed. C.-G. Yoo. Seoul: Cobook, 2003. Print.

Choe, C. *History of Korean Social Policy Research*. Seoul: Korea Institute of Social Security, 1991. Print.

Ch'oe, W. "Activities of Foreign Voluntary Agencies and Their Influences on Social Work Development in South Korea." Ph.D. Diss. Seoul National University, 1996. Print.

Choi, J. J. *Labor and the Authoritarian State: Labor Unions in South Korean Manufacturing Industries, 1961–1980*. Seoul: Korea University Press, 1989. Print.

Choi, J. J. *Labor Movement and the State in Korea*. Seoul: Nanam, 1997. Print.

Choi, Y., J. Kim, H. R. Cho, and B. S. Yu. *Korean Labor Movement since 1987*. Seoul: Korea Labor Institute, 2001. Print.

Chun, D. H. *Towards Peace and Prosperity: The President's Annual Summer Press Conference*. Seoul: Korea Overseas Information Service, 1984. Print.

Chun, I. *Park Chung Hee: A Commentary*. Seoul: Ihaksa, 2006. Print.

Chung, K. B., and I. S. Choi, eds. *Beyond Productive Welfare*, Seoul: Nanam, 2003. Print.

Chung, M.-K. "Rolling Back the Korean State: How Much Has Changed?" 2001 Meeting of the IPSA Section of Structure of Governance. University of Oklahoma. March 30–31, 2001. Print.

Chung, M.-K., ed. *Debate on the Nature of the Welfare State in Korea*, Vol. II. Seoul: Human and Welfare, 2009. Print.

Community Chest of Korea. *2002 Annual Report of the Community Chest of Korea*. Seoul: CCK, 2002. Print.

Council of Economic Organizations. *Survey on the Present Situation of Human Resource Department of Korean Companies*. Seoul: CEO, 1991. Print.

Clifford, M. L. *Troubled Tiger: Business, Bureaucrats and Generals in South Korea*. Armonk: M. E. Sharpe 1994. Print.

Cumings, B. *Korea's Place in the Sun: A Modern History*. New York: Norton, 2005. Print.

Dahl, R. A. *On Democracy*. New Haven: Yale University Press, 1998. Print.

Dahrendorf, R. "Challenges to the Voluntary Sector." 18th Arnold Goodman Lecture. London. 2001. Print.

Davies, N. *Europe: A History*. London: Pimlico, 1997. Print.

Deacon, B. *Global Social Policy and Governance*. London: Sage, 2007. Print.

Deakin, N. *In Search of Civil Society*. London: Palgrave, 2001. Print.

Demick, B. *Nothing to Envy: Real Lives in North Korea*. New York: Spiegel & Grau, 2010. Print.

Deyo, F. C. "Political Economy of Social Policy Formation: East Asia's Newly Industrialized Countries." *States and Development in the Asian Pacific Rim.* Eds. R. P. Appelbaum and J. Henderson. Newbury Park: Sage Publications, 1992. Print.

Diamond, L., and B.-K. Kim, eds. *Consolidating Democracy in South Korea,* Boulder: Lynne Rienner Publishers, 2000. Print.

DiMaggio, P., and W. W. Powell. "The Iron Cage Revisited: Institutional Isomorphism and Collective Rationality in Organizational Fields." *The New Institutionalism in Organizational Analysis.* Eds. W. W. Powell and P. DiMaggio. Chicago: University of Chicago Press, 1991. Print.

Doner, R. F., B. K. Ritchie, and D. Slater. "Systemic Vulnerability and the Origins of Developmental States: Northeast and Southeast Asia in Comparative Perspective." *International Organization* 59(2) (2005): 327–61. Print.

Durkheim, E. *The Division of Labor in Society.* New York: Free Press, 1997. Print.

Editorial Committee for the History of Korean Military Revolution. *The History of Korean Military Revolution* Vol. I–II. Seoul: Supreme Council for National Reconstruction, 1963. Print.

Eliaeson, S., ed. *Building Civil Society and Democracy in New Europe.* Newcastle: Cambridge Scholars Publishing, 2008. Print.

Estevez-Abe, M. *Welfare and Capitalism in Postwar Japan.* Cambridge: Cambridge University Press, 2008. Print.

Evans, P. B. *Embedded Autonomy: States and Industrial Transformation.* Princeton: Princeton University Press, 1995. Print.

Evers, A. "The Welfare Mix Approach: Understanding the Pluralism of Welfare Systems." *Balancing Pluralism: New Welfare Mixes in Care for the Elderly.* Eds. A. Evers and I. Svetlik. Aldershot: Avebury, 1993. Print.

Exworthy, M., and M. Powell. "Big Windows and Little Windows: Implementation in the 'Congested State.'" *Public Administration* 82(2) (2004): 263–81. Print.

Federation of Korean Industries. *The Survey on Actual Situation of Welfare in the Company.* Seoul: FKI, 1979. Print.

Federation of Korean Industries. *The White Paper of Charitable Giving of Corporate Foundations.* Seoul: FKI, 1998. Print.

Federation of Korean Trade Unions. *The History of Korean Trade Union Movements.* Seoul: FKTU, 1979. Print.

Finer, S. E. *The History of Government.* Vol. I–III. Oxford: Oxford University Press, 1997. Print.

Finlayson, G. "A Moving Frontier: Voluntarism and the State in British Social Welfare 1911–1949." *Twentieth Century British History* 1(2) (1990): 183–206. Print.

Flora, P., ed. *Growth to Limits: The Western European Welfare State since World War II.* Vol. I. Berlin: de Gruyter/European University Institute, 1986. Print.

Giddens, A. *The Third Way: The Renewal of Social Democracy.* Cambridge: Polity, 1998. Print.

Gilbert, N. "From 'Welfare' to 'Enabling' State." *Balancing Pluralism: New Welfare Mixes in Care for the Elderly.* Eds. A. Evers and I. Svetlik. Aldershot: Averbury, 1993. Print.

Glennerster, H. "Quasi-markets for Education?" *Economic Journal* 101 (1991): 1268–76. Print.

Goodman, R., G. White, and H.-J. Kwon, eds. *The East Asian Welfare Model: Welfare Orientalism and the State.* London: Routledge, 1998. Print.

Gough, I. "Globalization and Regional Welfare Regimes: The East Asian Case." *Global Social Policy* 1(2) (2001): 163–89. Print.

Gough, I. "East Asia: The Limits of Productivist Regimes." *Insecurity and Welfare Regimes in Asia, Africa and Latin America: Social Policy in Development Contexts.* Eds. I. Gough and G. Wood et al. Cambridge: Cambridge University Press, 2004. Print.

Gunther, J. *Inside Africa.* New York: Harper, 1955. Print.

Haggard, S. *Pathways from the Periphery.* Ithaca: Cornell University Press, 1990. Print.

Haggard, S. *The Political Economy of the Asian Financial Crisis.* Washington: Institute for International Economics, 2000. Print.

Haggard, S., and S. Collins. "The Political Economy of Adjustment in the 1980s." *Macroeconomic Policy and Adjustment in Korea 1970–1990.* Eds. S. Haggard, R. N. Cooper, S. Collins, C. Kim, and S.-T. Ro. Cambridge: Harvard Institute for International Development and Korean Development Institute, 1994. Print.

Haggard, S., and R. R. Kaufman. *Development, Democracy, and Welfare States: Latin American, East Asia, and Eastern Europe.* Princeton: Princeton University Press, 2008. Print.

Haggard, S., and C. I. Moon. "Institutions and Economic Policy: Theory and a Korean Case Study." *World Politics* 42(2) (1990): 210–37. Print.

Haggard, S., R. N. Cooper, S. Collins, C. Kim, and S.-T. Ro. *Macroeconomic Policy and Adjustment in Korea, 1970–1990.* Cambridge: Harvard Institute for International Development and Korean Development Institute, 1994. Print.

Hahn, S. and A. McCabe. "Welfare-to-Work and the Emerging Third Sector in South Korea: Korea's Third Way?" *International Journal of Social Welfare* 15(4) (2006): 314–20. Print.

Hall, P. A. and D. Soskice, eds. *Varieties of Capitalism: The Institutional Foundations of Comparative Advantage.* Oxford: Oxford University Press, 2001. Print.

Han, S. *The Failure of Democracy in South Korea.* Berkeley: University of California Press, 1974. Print.

Havel, V. "The Power of the Powerless." *The Power of the Powerless: Citizens Against the State in Central-Eastern Europe.* Ed. J. Keane. Armonk: M. E. Sharpe, 1985. Print.

Hill, M., and P. Hupe. *Implementing Public Policy: Governance in Theory and in Practice*. London: Sage, 2002. Print.

Holliday, I. "Productivist Welfare Capitalism: Social Policy in East Asia." *Political Studies* 48(4) (2000): 706–23. Print.

Holliday, I., and P. Wilding, eds. *Welfare Capitalism in East Asia: Social Policy in the Tiger Economies*. Basingstoke: Palgrave Macmillan, 2003. Print.

Hong, K. Z., and H. K. Song. "Continuity and Change in the Korean Welfare Regime." *Journal of Social Policy* 35(2) (2006): 247–65. Print.

Horowitz, I. L. *Behemoth: Main Currents in the History and Theory of Political Sociology*. New Brunswick: Transaction, 1999. Print.

Hort, S. "The Coming of East and Southeast Asian Welfare States." *Journal of European Social Policy* 10(2) (2000): 162–84. Print.

Hwang, C. S. "The Characteristics and Functions of Corporate Foundations." *East-West Studies* 10(2) (1998): 145–70. Print.

Hwang, D. S. "The Evaluation of Korea's Unemployment Benefits and the Challenges Ahead." International Seminar on Employment/Unemployment Insurance. Seoul. July 7–8, 2005. Print.

Hwang, G.-J. *Pathways to State Welfare in Korea: Interests, Ideas and Institutions*. Aldershot: Ashgate, 2006. Print.

Im, H. B. "The Rise of Bureaucratic Authoritarianism in South Korea." *World Politics* 39(2) (1987): 231–57. Print.

Im, H. B. "Changes in the Nature of the Korean State since the Independence." *Korean Politics in the 21st Century*. Ed. C. Lee. Seoul: Seoul National University Press, 2009. Print.

Im, Y. I. *Korean Labor Movement and Class Politics: 1987–1995*. Seoul: Kyungnam University Press, 1997. Print.

International Monetary Fund. *Republic of Korea—Request for Stand-by Arrangement*. EBS/97/222. Washington: IMF, 1997. Print.

Jacobs, D. "Low Public Expenditures on Social Welfare: Do East Asian Countries Have a Secret?" *International Journal of Social Welfare* 9(1) (2000): 2–16. Print.

John, M. "Social Protection in Southeast and East Asia—Towards a Comprehensive Picture." *Social Protection in Southeast and East Asia*. Eds. E. Adam, M. V. Hauff, and M. John. Singapore: Friedrich Ebert Stiftung, 2002. Print.

Johnson, N. *Mixed Economies of Welfare: A Comparative Perspective*. Hemel Hempstead: Simon & Schuster, 1999. Print.

Jones, C. "Hong Kong, Singapore, South Korea and Taiwan: Oikonomic Welfare States." *Government and Opposition* 25(4) (1990): 446–62. Print.

Jones, L., and I. Sakong. *Government, Business, and Entrepreneurship in Economic Development: The Korean Case*. Cambridge: Harvard University Press, 1980. Print.

Joo, J. "Dynamics of Social Policy Change: A Korean Case Study from a Comparative Perspective." *Governance* 12(1) (1999): 57–80. Print.

Kang, C., J. Choi, and J. Chang. *Chaebol*. Seoul: Bibong Publisher, 1991. Print.

Kang, K., Y. H. Lee, and S. Choi, eds. *The Policy Decision Making System during the Rapid Economic Growth in Korea: Economic Planning Board and Inter-Ministerial Committees*. Seoul: Korea Development Institute, 2008. Print.

Kendall, J., and M. Knapp. "A Loose and Baggy Monster: Boundaries, Definitions and Typologies." *An Introduction to the Voluntary Sector*. Eds. J. Davis-Smith, C. Rochester, and R. Hedley. London: Routledge, 1994. Print.

Keum, J. H. "Development Direction and Financial Prospect of the Employment Insurance." Forum for the Development and Financial Stabilization of the Employment Insurance. Seoul. May 10, 2005. Print.

Kim, D. J. *Prison Writings*. Berkeley: University of California Press, 1987. Print.

Kim, D. J. *Mass-Participatory Economy*. Cambridge: Centre for International Affairs, Harvard University, 1996. Print.

Kim, D. J. *Government of the People: Selected Speeches of President Kim Dae Jung*. Seoul: Office of the President, 1999. Print.

Kim, D. J. *Kim Dae Jung's Letters from Prison*. Seoul: Hanul, 2000. Print.

Kim E. M. "From Dominance to Symbiosis: State and Chaebol in Korea." *Pacific Focus* 3(2) (1988): 105–21. Print.

Kim, E. M. *Big Business, Strong State: Collusion and Conflict in South Korean Development, 1960–1990*, Albany: State University of New York Press, 1997. Print.

Kim, E. M., ed. *The Four Asian Tigers: Economic Development and the Global Political Economy*. San Diego: Academic Press, 1998. Print.

Kim, H.-A. *Korea's Development under Park Chung-Hee: Rapid Industrialization, 1961–79*. London: Routledge Curzon, 2004. Print.

Kim, H. K. *Political Economy of Korean Industrial Relations*. Seoul: Hanul, 1997. Print.

Kim, H.-R. "The State and Civil Society in Transition: The Role of Non-Governmental Organizations in South Korea." *The Pacific Review* 13(4) (2000): 595–613. Print.

Kim, I. "Memoires of Kim Ipsam." *Korea Economic Daily*. 12 October 1998. Print.

Kim, J. *Divided Korea: The Politics of Development 1945–1972*. Cambridge: Harvard University Press, 1976. Print.

Kim, J.-R. *A 30-Year History of Korean Economic Policy*. Seoul: Joong Ang Daily News, 1995. Print.

Kim, T. "Controlling the Welfare Mix: A Historical Review on the Changing Contours of State-Voluntary Relations in Korea." D.Phil. Diss. University of Oxford, 2007. Print.

Kim, T. "The Social Construction of Welfare Control: A Sociological Review on State-Voluntary Sector Links in Korea." *International Sociology* 23(6) (2008): 819–44. Print.

Kim, S. *The Politics of Democratization in Korea: The Role of Civil Society.* Pittsburgh: University of Pittsburgh Press, 2000. Print.

Kim, Y. G. and G. Yoo. *Wages in Korea.* Seoul: Korea Development Institute, 2000. Print.

Kim, Y.-M., ed. *Debate on the Nature of the Welfare State in Korea,* Vol. I. Seoul: Human and Welfare, 2002. Print.

Kim, Y.-M. "Beyond East Asian Welfare Productivism in South Korea." *Policy and Politics* 36(1) (2008): 109–25. Print.

Kim, Y. "The Size and Conditions of Non-Regular Employment", *Monthly Bulletin for Labor & Society,* Vol. 137, (2008) Korea Labor & Society Institute. Print.

Kim, Y. S. *Korea's Quest for Reform & Globalization: Selected Speeches of President Kim Young Sam.* Seoul: Office of the President, 1995. Print.

King, D., and S. Wood. "The Political Economy of Neoliberalism: Britain and the United States in the 1980s." *Continuity and Change in Contemporary Capitalism.* Eds. H. Kitschelt, P. Lange, G. Marks, and J. D. Stephens. Cambridge: Cambridge University Press, 1999. Print.

Kingdon, J. *Agendas, Alternatives and Public Policies.* Boston: Little Brown, 1984. Print.

Kohli, A. *State-Directed Development: Political Power and Industrialization in the Global Periphery.* New York: Cambridge University Press, 2004. Print.

Koo, H. "Strong State and Contentious Society." *State and Society in Contemporary Korea.* Ed. H. Koo. Ithaca: Cornell University Press, 1993. Print.

Koo, H. *Korean Workers: The Culture and Politics of Class Formation.* Ithaca: Cornell University Press, 2001. Print.

Korea Employers Federation. *The 20 Years History of the Korea Employers Federation.* Seoul: KEF, 1990. Print.

Korea Institute for Health and Social Affairs. *A Study on Ways to Fill Gaps in the Coverage of Social Insurance.* Seoul: KIHASA, 2005. Print.

Korea Labor Institute. *Labor-Management Relations and Labor Politics in Korea,* Vol. I. Seoul: KLI, 1999. Print.

Korea Labor Institute. *Evaluation and Development Direction of the Employment Insurance System,* Seoul: KLI, 2000. Print.

Korean Association of Voluntary Agencies. *The History of Foreign Voluntary Agencies: The Forty-Year History of the KAVA.* Seoul: Hongikche, 1995. Print.

Ku, Y.-W. *Welfare Capitalism in Taiwan: State, Economy and Social Policy.* London: Macmillan, 1997. Print.

Kuhnle, S., and P. Selle. "Government and Voluntary Organizations: A Relational Perspective." *Government and Voluntary Organizations: A Relational Perspective.* Eds. S. Kuhnle and P. Selle. Aldershot: Avebury, 1992. Print.

Kwon, H.-J. "Beyond European Welfare Regimes: Comparative Perspectives on East Asian Welfare Systems." *Journal of Social Policy* 26(4) (1997): 467–84. Print.

Kwon, H.-J. *The Welfare State in Korea: The Politics of Legitimation*. London: Macmillan, 1999. Print.

Kwon, H.-J. "Globalization, Unemployment and Policy Responses in Korea: Repositioning the State?" *Global Social Policy* 1(2) (2001): 213–34. Print.

Kwon, H.-J. "Advocacy Coalitions and the Politics of Welfare in Korea after the Economic Crisis." *Policy and Politics* 31(1) (2003): 69–83. Print.

Kwon, H.-J. "The Economic Crisis and the Politics of Welfare Reform in Korea." *Social Policy in a Developmental Context*. Ed. T. Mkandawire. Basingstoke: Palgrave Macmillan, 2004. Print.

Kwon, H.-J., ed. *Transforming the Developmental Welfare State in East Asia*. Basingstoke: Palgrave Macmillan, 2005. Print.

Kwon, H.-J. "The Reform of the Developmental Welfare State in East Asia." *International Journal of Social Welfare* 18(s1) (2009a): 12–21. Print.

Kwon, H.-J. "Korea: Rescaling the Developmental Welfare State?" *International Social Policy: Welfare Regimes in the Developed World*. Eds. P. Alcock and G. Craig. Basingstoke: Palgrave Macmillan, 2009b. Print.

Kwon, H.-J. and Yi, I. "Economic Development and Poverty Reduction in Korea: Governing Multifunctional Institutions." *Development and Change* 40(4) (2009): 769–92. Print.

Kwon, S. "Social Policies in Korea: Challenges and Responses." Seoul: Korea Development Institute. 1993. Research Monograph, 93-01. Print.

Kwon, S. "The Korean Experience of Poverty Reduction: Lessons and Prospects." *Poverty Alleviation*. Ed. Korea Development Institute/United Nations Development Programme. Seoul: Korea Development Institute, 1998. Print.

Kwon, S., and M. O'Donnell. *Chaebol and Labour in Korea: Development of Management Strategy in Hyundai*. London: Routledge, 2001. Print.

Labor-Management-Government Commission. *Discussion Material for the Plan for Upgrading the Employment Service*, Seoul: Labor-Management-Government Commission, 2004. Print.

Le Grand, J. and W. Bartlett. "Quasi-Markets and Social Policy: The Way Forward?" *Quasi-Markets and Social Policy*. Eds. J. Le Grand and W. Bartlett. London: Macmillan, 1993. Print.

Leat, D. "Are Voluntary Organisations Accountable?" *Voluntary Agencies: Challenges of Organisation and Management*. Eds. D. Billis and M. Harris. London: Macmillan, 1996. Print.

Lee, B.-C., ed. *Developmental Dictatorship and the Park Chung-Hee Era: The Shaping of Modernity in the Republic of Korea*. Paramus: Homa & Sekey Books, 2006. Print.

Lee, B. H., and B. S. Yoo. "The Republic of Korea: From Flexibility to Segmentation." *Globalization, Flexibilization and Working Conditions in Asia and the Pacific*. Eds. S. Lee and F. Eyraud. Oxford: Chandos Publishing, 2009. Print.

Lee, H.-B. *Korea: Time, Change and Administration*. Honolulu: East-West Centre Press, 1968. Print.

Lee, H. K. "Historical and Structural Characteristics of Korea's Nonprofit Welfare Sector." *East-West Studies* 10(2) (1998): 41–75. Print.

Lee, H. K. "Globalization and the Emerging Welfare State—The Experience of South Korea." *International Journal of Social Welfare* 8(1) (1999): 23–37. Print.

Lee, J. "Welfare Reform in Korea after the Economic Crisis." D.Phil. Diss. University of Oxford, 2008. Print.

Lee, J. "Another Dimension of Welfare Reform: The Implementation of the Employment Insurance Programme in Korea." *International Journal of Social Welfare.* 18(3) (2009): 281–90. Print.

Lee, J., and Rhee, C. "Social Impacts of the Asian Crisis: Policy Challenges and Lessons." Human Development Report Occasional Paper 33, Geneva: UNDP, 1999. Print.

Lee, K. "Political Legitimacy of the Third Republic and the Park Government." *Korean Political Science Review* 31(4) (1997): 89–108. Print.

Lee, K. K. "The Change of the Financial System and Developmental State in Korea." 1998. Monograph, http://www.ritsumei.ac.jp/~leekk/study/change-e. doc.

Lee, S., and F. Eyraud, eds. *Globalization, Flexibilization and Working Conditions in Asia and the Pacific.* Oxford: Chandos Publishing, 2009. Print.

Lee, Y. "Participatory Democracy and Chaebol Regulation in Korea: State-Market Relations under the MDG Governments, 1997–2003." *Asian Survey* 45(2) (2005): 279–301. Print.

Lewis, N. "Corporatism and Accountability: The Democratic Dilemma." *Corporatism and Accountability: Organized Interests in British Public Life.* Eds. C. Crouch and R. Dore. Oxford: Oxford University Press, 1990. Print.

Lijphart, A. *Patterns of Democracy: Government Forms and Performance in Thirty-Six Countries.* New Haven: Yale University Press, 1999. Print.

Lim, H., and S. Kong. "Social Justice and Welfare Movement Organizations." *The Sociology of New Social Movement.* Eds. T. Kwon et al. Seoul: Seoul National University Press, 2001. Print.

Lim, H.-C. *Dependent Development in South Korea, 1963–1979.* Seoul: Seoul National University Press, 1985. Print.

Lipsky, M. *Street-level Bureaucracy: Dilemmas of the Individual in Public Services.* New York: Russell Sage Foundation, 1980. Print.

Martin, J. P. "What Works among Active Labour Market Policies: Evidence from OECD Countries' Experiences." Labour Market and Social Policy—Occasional Papers No. 35. Paris: OECD. 1998. Print.

Mayhew, S. H. "Hegemony, Politics and Ideology: The Role of Legislation in NGO-Government Relations in Asia." *Journal of Development Studies* 41(5) (2005): 727–58. Print.

McNamara, D. L., ed. *Corporatism and Korean Capitalism.* London: Routledge, 1999. Print.

Meyer, J. W., and B. Rowan. "Institutionalized Organizations: Formal Structure as Myth and Ceremony." *American Journal of Sociology* 83(2) (1977): 340–63. Print.

Ministry of Government Administration and Home Affairs. *2000 Financial Yearbook of Local Government.* Seoul: MOGAHA, 2000. Print.

Ministry of Government Administration and Home Affairs. *White Paper of Government Administration and Home Affairs.* Seoul: MOGAHA, 2002. Print.

Ministry of Health and Welfare [Annual]. *Health and Welfare Statistical Yearbook,* Kwacheon: MOHW. Print.

Ministry of Health and Social Affairs. *White Paper of Health and Social Affairs.* Kwacheon: MOHSA, 1985, 1992. Print.

Ministry of Health and Welfare. *White Paper of Reforms of Restrictions on Health and Social Welfare.* Kwacheon: MOHW, 1999. Print.

Ministry of Health and Welfare. *2001 Handbook of the National Basic Livelihood Security System.* Kwacheon: MOHW, 2001a. Print.

Ministry of Health and Welfare. *Policy Directions for Improving the National Basic Livelihood Security System.* Kwacheon: MOHW, 2001b. Print.

Ministry of Health and Welfare. *White Paper of Health and Welfare.* Kwacheon: MOHW, 2002, 2005. Print.

Ministry of Home Affairs. *Saemaul Movement: From the Beginning to the Present.* Seoul: MOHA, 1973. Print.

Ministry of Home Affairs. *10 Years of History of the New Community Movement.* Seoul: MOHA, 1980. Print.

Ministry of Labor. *Unemployment Measure White Paper: 1998–2000.* Kwacheon: MOL, 2001. Print.

Ministry of Labor. "Plan for Upgrading the Employment Assistance Service." Report Meeting for the Reform of the National Employment Assistance Service. Seoul. April 6, 2005. Paper. Print.

Ministry of Planning and Budget. *A Trend of Social Welfare Restructuring in Major Countries.* Seoul: MOPB, 1999. Print.

Mishra, R., S. Kuhnle, N. Gilbert, and K. B. Chung, eds. *Modernizing the Korean Welfare State: Towards the Productive Welfare Model.* Brunswick: Transaction Publisher, 2004. Print.

Mkandawire, T., ed. *Social Policy in a Developmental Context.* Basingstoke: Palgrave Macmillan, 2004. Print.

Mommsen, W. S., ed. *The Emergence of the Welfare State in Britain and Germany.* London: Croom Helm, 1981. Print.

Moore, B. Jr. *Social Origins of Dictatorship and Democracy: Lord and Peasant in the Making of the Modern World.* Boston: Beacon Press, 1966. Print.

Mosley, H., T. Keller, and S. Speckesser. "The Role of the Social Partners in the Design and Implementation of Active Measures." Employment and Training Papers 27. Geneva: International Labour Organization. 1998. Print.

Nam, H. *Building Ships, Building a Nation: Korea's Democratic Unionism under Park Chung Hee.* Seattle: University of Washington Press, 2009. Print.

National Association for Disaster Relief. *The Twenty-Year History of the National Association for Disaster Relief,* Seoul: NADR, 1987. Print.

Nye, J. S. *The Powers to Lead.* New York: Oxford University Press, 2008. Print.

Office of Labor Affairs. *Yearbook of Labor Statistics,* Seoul: OLA, 1980. Print.

Office of the President. *President Park Chung Hee's Selected Speeches: Saemaul Movement,* Seoul: OP, 1978. Print.

Office of the President. *The Productive Welfare towards New Millennium,* Seoul: OP, 1999. Print.

Oh, J. K.-C. *Korea: Democracy on Trial.* Ithaca: Cornell University Press, 1968. Print.

Oh, J. K.-C. *Korean Politics: The Quest for Democratization and Economic Development.* Ithaca: Cornell University Press, 1999. Print.

Oh, K. H. "Korean Chaebols." *Human and Social Science* 20 (1975): 207–32. Print.

Oh, Y. S. "Park Chung-Hee's Modernization Strategy and Rural Saemaul Movement." *Trends and Prospects* 55(4) (2002): 157–77. Print.

Oniz, Z. "The Logic of the Developmental State." *Comparative Politics* 24(1) (1991): 109–26. Print.

Organisation for Economic Co-operation and Development (OECD). *Pushing Ahead with Reform in Korea: Labour Market and Social Safety-net Policies.* Paris: Organisation for Economic Co-operation and Development, 2000. Print.

OECD. *OECD Employment Outlook.* Paris: Organisation for Economic Co-operation and Development, 2005. Print.

O'Toole, L. J. Jr. "Research on Policy Implementation: Assessment and Prospects." *Journal of Public Administration Research and Theory* 10(2) (2000): 263–88. Print.

Paek, C. "A Study of Shared Roles between the State and Voluntarism in Social Welfare Services." Ph.D. Diss. Seoul National University, 1994. Print.

Park, C. H. *The Country, Revolution and I.* Seoul: Hollym, 1963. Print.

Park, C. H. *The Country, Revolution and I. 2nd edition,* Seoul: Hollym, 1970. Print.

Park, T., K. Jung, S. W. Sokolowski, and L. M. Salamon. "South Korea." *Global Civil Society: Dimensions of the Nonprofit Sector.* Eds. L. M. Salamon et al. Bloomfield: Kumarian Press, 2004. Print.

Park, Y. C. "Price Control and Stabilization Measures." *Economic Development in the Republic of Korea: A Policy Perspective.* Eds. L. Cho and Y. H. Kim. Hawaii: East-West Center, 1991. Print.

Peng, I. "Post-industrial Pressures, Political Regime Shifts, and Social Policy Reform in Japan and South Korea." *Journal of East Asian Studies* 4(3) (2004): 389–425. Print.

Pierson, P., ed. *The New Politics of the Welfare State.* Oxford: Oxford University Press, 2001. Print.

Piven, F., and R. Cloward. *Regulating the Poor: The Functions of Public Welfare.* New York: Pantheon Books, 1971. Print.

Piven, F., and R. Cloward. *Poor People's Movements: Why They Succeed, How They Fail.* New York: Vintage Books, 1979. Print.

Presidential Committee for Quality of Life. *The Way of Productive Welfare for the New Millennium.* Seoul: Office of the President, 1999. Print.

Presidential Commission on Policy Planning. *Policy Directions for Establishing Productive Welfare to Prepare for a Knowledge-based Information Society in the 21st Century.* Seoul: PCPP, 1999. Print.

Presidential Committee on the Globalization Campaign. *Prospects and Strategies for Globalization.* Seoul: Seoul Press, 1995. Print.

Presidential Committee on the Globalization Campaign. *White Paper of the Globalization Campaign.* Seoul: PCGC, 1998. Print.

Ramesh, M. *Welfare Capitalism in Southeast Asia.* London: Macmillan, 2000. Print.

Ramesh, M. "Globalization and Social Security Expansion in East Asia." *States in the Global Economy: Bringing Domestic Institutions Back In.* Ed. L. Weiss. New York: Cambridge University Press, 2003. Print.

Reeve, W. D. *The Republic of Korea: A Political and Economic Study.* London: Oxford University Press, 1963. Print.

Rimlinger, G. V. *Welfare Policy and Industrialization in Europe, America, and Russia.* New York: Wiley, 1971. Print.

Ringen, S. *The Possibility of Politics.* 3rd edition, New Brunswick: Transaction Publishers, 2006. Print.

Ringen, S. *What Democracy Is For: On Freedom and Moral Government.* Princeton: Princeton University Press, 2007. Print.

Ringen, S. "The Powerlessness of Powerful Government." *Building Civil Society and Democracy in New Europe.* Ed. S. Eliaeson. Newcastle: Cambridge Scholars Publishing, 2008. Print.

Ringen, S. *The Economic Consequences of Mr. Brown: How a Strong Government Was Defeated by a Weak System of Governance.* Oxford: Bardwell Press, 2009. Print.

Roh, T. W. *Korea: A Nation Transformed: Selected Speeches of Roh Tae Woo, President of the Republic of Korea.* Oxford: Pergamon Press, 1990. Print.

Rose, R. "Common Goals but Different Roles: The State's Contribution to the Welfare Mix." *The Welfare State East and West.* Eds. R. Rose and R. Shiratori. Oxford: Oxford University Press, 1986. Print.

Salamon, L. M. *Partners in Public Services: Government-Nonprofit Relations in the Modern Welfare State.* Baltimore: Johns Hopkins University Press, 1995. Print.

Salamon, L. M., and H. Anheier, eds. *Defining the Nonprofit Sector: A Cross-National Analysis*. Manchester: Manchester University Press, 1997. Print.

Satterwhite, D. H. "The Politics of Economic Development: Coup, State, and the Republic of Korea's First Five-Year Economic Development Plan (1962–1966)." Ph.D. Diss. University of Washington, 1994. Print.

Seong, K.-R. "Preparing for the Post-IMF System: In Search of a New Model for National Development and Social Integration." *The Korea Public Administration Journal* 10(2) (2001): 260–90. Print.

Shin, D. C. *Mass Politics and Culture in Democratizing Korea*, Cambridge: Cambridge University Press, 1999. Print.

Shin, D.-M. *Social and Economic Policies in Korea: Ideas, Networks and Linkages*. London: RoutledgeCurzon, 2003. Print.

Sohn, H. *Authoritarianism and Oppression in South Korea*. London: Routledge, 1989. Print.

Son, J. *A Study of the Policy Process of Social Policy Making in Korea*. Ph.D. Diss. Seoul National University, 1981. Print.

Soskice, D. "Divergent Production Regimes: Coordinated and Uncoordinated Market Economies in the 1980s and 1990s." *Continuity and Change in Contemporary Capitalism*. Eds. H. Kitschelt, P. Lange, G. Marks, and J. D. Stephens. Cambridge: Cambridge University Press, 1999. Print.

Stern, J. J., J. Kim, D. H. Perkins, and J. Yoo. *Industrialization and the State: The Korean Heavy and Chemical Industry Drive*. Cambridge: Harvard Institute for International Development, 1995. Print.

Streeck, W. "The Study of Organized Interests: Before 'The Century' and After." *The Diversity of Democracy: Corporatism, Social Order and Political Conflict*. Eds. C. Crouch and W. Streeck. Cheltenham: Edward Elgar, 2006. Print.

Tang, K.-L. *Social Welfare Development in East Asia*. New York: Palgrave, 2000. Print.

Taylor, C. *Philosophical Arguments*. Cambridge: Harvard University Press, 1995. Print.

Tsebelis, G. *Veto Players: How Political Institutions Work*. Princeton: Princeton University Press, 2002. Print.

Wade, R. *Governing the Market*, Princeton: Princeton University Press, 1990. Print.

Wade, R., and F. Veneroso. "The Asian Crisis: The High Debt Model Versus the Wall Street-Treasury-IMF Complex." *New Left Review* 228 (1998): 3–23. Print.

Walker, A., and C.-K. Wong, eds. *East Asian Welfare Regimes in Transition: From Confucianism to Globalisation*. Bristol: The Policy Press, 2005. Print.

Ware, A. *Between Profit and State: Intermediate Organizations in Britain and the United States*. Cambridge: Polity, 1989. Print.

Weiss, L., ed. *States in the Global Economy: Bringing Domestic Institutions Back In.* New York: Cambridge University Press, 2003. Print.

Whang, I. J. *Management of Rural Change in Korea: The Saemaul Undong.* Seoul: Seoul National University Press, 1981. Print.

White, G., and R. Goodman. "Welfare Orientalism and the Search for an East Asian Welfare Model." *The East Asian Welfare Model: Welfare Orientalism and the State.* Eds. R. Goodman, G. White, and H.-J. Kwon. London: Routledge, 1998. Print.

Whitehead, L. "Democratization and Social Policy." *Social Policy in a Development Context.* Ed. T. Mkandawire. London: Palgrave, 2004. Print.

Wiarda, H. J. *Corporatism and Comparative Politics: The Other Great "Ism".* Armonk: M. E. Sharpe, 1997. Print.

Wolch, J. *The Shadow State: Government and Voluntary Sector in Transition.* New York: Foundation Center, 1990. Print.

Wong, J. *Healthy Democracies: Welfare Politics in Taiwan and South Korea.* Ithaca: Cornell University Press, 2004. Print.

Woo, J. *Race to the Swift: State and Finance in Korean Industrialization.* New York: Columbia University Press, 1991. Print.

Woo, M. *The Politics of Social Welfare Policy in South Korea: Growth and Citizenship.* Lanham: University Press of America, 2004. Print.

Woo-Cumings, M., ed. *The Developmental State.* Ithaca: Cornell University Press, 1999. Print.

Yang, P., G. Lee, and J. Kim. *A Study of Improving Workers' Housing.* Seoul: Institute of Labor Economics, Korea Employers Federation, 1990. Print.

Yang, Y. "Work in Later Life: Examining the Impact of Post-Retirement Work on Economic Wellbeing and Social Inclusion in Korea." D.Phil. Diss. University of Oxford, 2010. Print.

Yi, I. *The Politics of Occupational Welfare in Korea.* Fukuoka: Hana-Syoin Press, 2007. Print.

Yi, I., and B. H. Lee. "Development Strategies and Unemployment Policies in Korea." *Transforming the Developmental Welfare State in East Asia.* Ed. H.-J. Kwon. Basingstoke: Palgrave Macmillan, 2005. Print.

Yi, Y. "Welfare Policies and Discourses of Social Discrimination and Exclusion." *Social Policy and Discourse of Integration and Exclusion.* Ed. Y. Yi. Seoul: Cobook, 2003. Print.

Yi, Y. "The Developmental Process of Social Welfare Movements." *Korea's Social Welfare Movements.* Ed. Y. Yi. Seoul: Human and Welfare, 2005. Print.

INDEX

135